The Spirit of Love

By: William Law

The Spirit of Love

Part One

In a letter to a friend

My Dear Friend,

[Love-1-1] YOU had no Occasion to make any Apology for the Manner of your Letter to me, for though you very well know that I have as utter an aversion to waste my Time and Thoughts in Matters of theological Debate as in any Contentions merely of a worldly Nature, as knowing that the Former are generally as much, if not more, hurtful to the Heart of Man than the Latter; yet as your Objections rather tend to stir up the Powers of Love than the wrangle of a rational Debate, so I consider them only as Motives and Occasions of edifying both you and myself with the Truth, the Power and Divine Blessedness of the *Spirit of Love*.

[Love-1-2] You say 'There is nothing in all my Writings that has more affected you than that Spirit of Love that breathes in them, and that you wish for nothing so much as to have a *living Sensibility* of the Power, Life, and Religion of Love. But you have these two Objections often rising in your Mind: *First*, that this Doctrine of pure and universal Love may be too refined and imaginary, because you find that however you like it, yet you cannot attain to it, or overcome all That in your Nature which is contrary to it, do what you can; and so are only able to be an Admirer of that Love which you cannot lay hold of. *Secondly*, Because you find so much said in Scripture of a *Righteousness* and *Justice*, a *Wrath* and *Vengeance* of God that must be *atoned* and *satisfied*, &c., that though you are in Love with that Description of the Deity which I have given, as a Being that is *all Love*, yet you have some Doubt whether the Scripture will allow of it.'

[Love-1-3] Thus stand your Objections, which will fall into nothing as soon as you look at them from a right Point of View, Which will then be, as soon as you have found the true Ground of the Nature, Power, and Necessity of the blessed Spirit of Love.

[Love-1-4] Now the Spirit of Love has this Original. God, as considered in himself in his Holy Being, before any thing is brought forth by him or out of him, is only an *eternal Will to all Goodness*. This is the *one eternal immutable* God, that from Eternity to Eternity changeth not, that can be neither more nor less nor any thing else but an *eternal Will to all the Goodness* that is in himself, and can come from him. The Creation of ever so many Worlds or *System*s of Creatures adds nothing to, nor takes any thing from this immutable God. He always was and always will be the same *immutable Will to all Goodness*. So that as certainly as he is the Creator, so certainly is he the Blesser of every created Thing, and can give *nothing* but Blessing, Goodness, and Happiness from himself because he has *in himself* nothing else to give. It is much more possible for the Sun to give forth Darkness, than for God to do, or be, or give forth anything but Blessing and Goodness. Now this is the *Ground and Original* of the Spirit of Love in the Creature; it is and must be a *Will to all Goodness*, and you have not the *Spirit of Love* till you have this Will to all Goodness at all Times and on all Occasions. You may indeed do many Works of Love and delight in them, especially at such Times as they are not inconvenient to you, or contradictory to your State or Temper or Occurrences in Life. But the Spirit of Love is not in you till it is the Spirit of your Life, till you live *freely, willingly, and universally* according to it. For every Spirit acts with Freedom and Universality according to what it is. It needs no command to live its *own Life*, or be what it is, no more than you need bid Wrath be wrathful. And therefore when *Love* is the Spirit of your Life, it will have the *Freedom* and *Universality* of a Spirit; it will always live and work in Love, not because of *This* or *That*, *Here* or *There*, but because the Spirit of Love can only love, wherever it is or goes or whatever is done to it. As the *Sparks* know no Motion but that of flying upwards, whether it be in the Darkness of the Night or in the Light of the Day, so the Spirit of Love is always in the same Course; it knows no Difference of Time, Place, or Persons, but whether it *gives* or *forgives*, *bears* or *forbears*, it is equally doing its own delightful Work, equally blessed from itself. For the Spirit of Love, wherever it is, is its own Blessing and Happiness because it is the *Truth* and *Reality* of God in the Soul, and therefore is in the same Joy of Life and is the same Good to itself, everywhere and on every Occasion.

[Love-1-5] Oh Sir! Would you know the Blessing of all Blessings? It is this *God of Love* dwelling in your Soul and killing every Root of Bitterness which is the Pain and Torment of every earthly, selfish Love. For all Wants are satisfied, all Disorders of Nature are removed, no Life is any longer a Burden, every Day is a Day of Peace, every thing you meet becomes a Help to you because every thing you see or do is all done in the sweet, gentle Element of Love. For as Love has no By-Ends, wills nothing but its *own Increase*, so every thing is as Oil to its Flame. It must have that which it wills and cannot be disappointed, because every thing naturally helps it to live in its *own Way* and to bring forth its *own Work*. The Spirit of Love does not want to be rewarded, honoured, or esteemed. Its only Desire is to propagate itself and become the Blessing and Happiness of every thing that wants it. And therefore it meets Wrath and Evil and Hatred and Opposition with the same *one Will* as the Light meets the Darkness, only to overcome it with all its Blessings. Did you want to avoid the Wrath and Ill-will or to gain the Favour of any Persons, you might easily miss of your Ends; but if you have no Will but to *all Goodness*, everything you meet, be it what it Will, must be forced to be assistant to you. For the Wrath of an Enemy, the Treachery of a Friend, and every other Evil only helps the Spirit of Love to be more triumphant, to live its *own Life* and find all its own Blessings in a higher Degree. Whether therefore you consider *Perfection* or *Happiness*, it is all included in the Spirit of Love and must be so for this Reason, because the infinitely perfect and happy God is mere Love, an *unchangeable Will to all Goodness*; and therefore every Creature must be corrupt and unhappy, so far as it is led by any other Will than the *one Will to all Goodness*. Thus you see the Ground, the Nature, and Perfection of the Spirit of Love. Let me now in a Word or two show you the Necessity of it. Now the Necessity is absolute and unchangeable. No Creature can be a Child of God but because the Goodness of God is in it; nor can it have any Union or Communion with the Goodness of the Deity till its Life is a Spirit of Love. This is the one only Band of Union betwixt God and the Creature. All besides this, or that is not this, call it by what Name you Will, is only so much Error, Fiction, Impurity, and Corruption got into the Creature, and must of all Necessity be entirely separated from it before it can have that Purity and Holiness which alone can see God or find the Divine Life. For as God is an *immutable Will* to all Goodness, so the Divine Will can unite or Work with no creaturely Will but that which willeth with him only that which is good. Here the Necessity is absolute; nothing will do instead of this Will; all Contrivances of Holiness, all Forms of religious Piety, signify nothing without this *Will to all Goodness*. For as the Will to all Goodness is the *whole Nature* of God, so it must be the *whole Nature* of every Service or Religion that can be acceptable to him. For nothing serves God or worships and adores him but that which wills and worketh with him. For God can Delight in nothing but his *own Will* and his *own Spirit*, because all Goodness is included in it and can be nowhere else. And therefore every thing that followeth an *own Will* or an *own Spirit* forsaketh the *one Will* to all Goodness, and whilst it doth so, hath no Capacity for the Light and Spirit of God. The Necessity therefore of *the Spirit of Love* is what God himself cannot dispense with in the Creature, no more than he can deny himself or act contrary to his own holy Being. But as it was his *Will to all Goodness* that brought forth Angels and the Spirits of Men, so he can Will nothing in their Existence but that they should live and work and manifest that *same Spirit* of Love and Goodness which brought them into Being. Every thing therefore but the *Will* and *Life* of Goodness is an *Apostasy* in the Creature and is Rebellion against the *whole Nature* of God.

[Love-1-6] There is no Peace, nor ever can be for the Soul of Man but in the Purity and Perfection of its first created Nature; nor can it have its Purity and Perfection in any other Way than in and by the *Spirit of Love*. For as Love is the God that created all Things, so Love is the Purity, the Perfection, and Blessing of all created Things; and nothing can live in God but as it lives in Love. Look at every Vice, Pain, and Disorder in human Nature; it is in itself nothing else but the Spirit of the Creature turned from the *Universality* of Love to some *self-seeking* or *own Will* in created Things. So that Love alone is, and only can be, the Cure of every Evil, and he that lives in the Purity of Love is risen out of the Power of Evil into the Freedom of the one Spirit of Heaven. The *Schools* have given us very accurate Definitions of every Vice, whether it be Covetousness, Pride, Wrath, Envy, &c., and shown us how to conceive them as *notionally* distinguished from one another. But the Christian has a much shorter Way of knowing their Nature and Power and what they all are and do in and to himself. For call them by what Names you will, or distinguish them with ever so much Exactness, they are all, separately and jointly, just that *same one* Thing, and all do that *same one Work* as the Scribes, the Pharisees, Hypocrites, and Rabble of the *Jews* who crucified Christ were all but *one and the same Thing* and all did *one and the same Work*, however different they were in outward Names. If you would therefore have a true Sense of the Nature and Power of Pride, Wrath, Covetousness, Envy, &c., they are in their whole Nature nothing else but the *Murderers* and *Crucifiers* of the true Christ of God; not as the High-Priests did many hundred Years ago, nailing his outward Humanity to an outward Cross, but crucifying afresh the Son of God, the holy *Immanuel*, who is the Christ that every Man crucifies as often as he gives way to Wrath, Pride, Envy, or Covetousness, *&c.* For every Temper or Passion that is contrary to the new Birth of Christ and keeps the holy Immanuel from coming to Life *in the Soul* is, in the strictest Truth of the Words, a *Murderer* and *Killer* of the Lord of Life. And where Pride and Envy and Hatred, *&c.*, are suffered to live, there the same Thing is done as when Christ was killed and Barrabas was saved alive. The Christ of God was not then first crucified when the Jews brought him to the Cross but *Adam* and *Eve* were his first real Murderers; for the Death which happened to them in the Day that they did eat of the earthly Tree was the Death of the Christ of God or the Divine Life in their Souls. For Christ had never come into the World as a second *Adam* to redeem it had he not been originally the *Life* and *Perfection* and *Glory* of the First *Adam*. And he is our Atonement and Reconciliation with God, because by and through him brought to Life *in us*, we are set again in that *first State* of Holiness, and have Christ *again* in us as our first Father had at his Creation. For had not Christ been in our first Father as a *Birth of Life* in him, *Adam* had been created a mere Child of *Wrath*, in the same *Impurity* of Nature, in the same *Enmity* with God, and in the same *Want* of an atoning Saviour as we are at this Day.— For God can have no Delight or Union with any Creature but because his well-beloved Son, the express Image of his Person, is *found* in it.— This is as true of all unfallen as of all fallen Creatures; the one are redeemed and the other want no Redemption, only through the Life of Christ dwelling *in them*. For as the Word, or Son of God, is the Creator of all Things, and by him every Thing is made that was made, so every Thing that is *good* and *holy* in unfallen Angels is as much through his *living* and *dwelling* in them as every Thing that is good and holy in *redeemed* Man is through him. And he is just as much the *preserver*, the *Strength, and Glory, and Life* of all the Thrones and Principalities of Heaven as he is the Righteousness, the Peace, and Redemption of fallen Man.

[Love-1-7] This Christ of God hath many Names in Scripture, but they all mean only this, that he is, and alone can be, the *Light* and *Life* and *Holiness* of every Creature that is holy, whether in Heaven or on Earth. Wherever Christ is not, there is the *Wrath* of Nature or Nature left to itself and its own tormenting Strength of Life, to feel nothing in itself but the vain, restless Contrariety of its own working Properties. This is the one only Origin of Hell, and every kind of Curse and Misery in the Creature. It is Nature without the Christ of God or the *Spirit of Love* ruling over it. And here you may observe that *Wrath* has in itself the Nature of Hell, and that it can have no Beginning or Power in any Creature but *so far* as it has lost the Christ of God. And when Christ is *everywhere*, Wrath and Hatred Will be *nowhere*. Whenever therefore you *willingly* indulge Wrath or let your Mind *work* in Hatred, you not only work *without* Christ, but you *resist* him and *withstand* his redeeming Power over you. You do in Reality what those *Jews* did when they said, "We will not have this Man to reign over us." For Christ never was, nor can be, in any Creature but purely as *a Spirit of Love*.

[Love-1-8] In all the Universe of Nature nothing but Heaven and heavenly Creatures ever had, or could have, been known, had every created Will continued in that State in which it came forth out of and from God. For God can will nothing in the Life of the Creature but a creaturely Manifestation of his own *Goodness, Happiness and Perfection*. And therefore, where this is wanted, the Fact is certain that the Creature hath *changed* and *lost* its first State that it had from God. Every Thing therefore which is the *Vanity*, the *Wrath*, the *Torment* and Evil of Man or any intelligent Creature is solely the Effect of his Will *turned* from God and can come from nothing else. Misery and Wickedness can have no other Ground or Root, for whatever wills and works with God must of all Necessity partake of the Happiness and Perfection of God.

[Love-1-9] This therefore is a certain Truth, that Hell and Death, Curse and Misery, can never cease or be removed from the Creation till the *Will of the Creature is again* as it came from God and is only *a Spirit of Love* that willeth nothing but Goodness. All the whole fallen Creation, stand it never so long, must groan and travail in Pain; this must be its *Purgatory* till every *Contrariety* to the Divine Will is *entirely* taken from every Creature.

[Love-1-10] Which is only saying that all the Powers and Properties of Nature are a Misery to themselves, can only Work in Disquiet and Wrath till the *Birth of the Son of God* brings them under the Dominion and Power of the *Spirit of Love*.

[Love-1-11] Thus Sir, you have seen the Original, immutable Ground and Necessity of the Spirit of Love. It is no imaginary Refinement or speculative Curiosity, but is of the highest Reality and most absolute Necessity. It stands in the *Immutability* and *Perfection* of God, and not only every intelligent Creature, be it what and where it will, but every inanimate Thing must work in *Vanity* and *Disquiet* till it has *its State in* and works under, the Spirit of Love. For as Love brought forth all Things, and all Things were what they were and had their Place and State under the *working Power* of Love, so every Thing that has *lost* its first-created State must be in restless Strife and Disquiet till it finds it again. There is no sort of Strife, Wrath, or Storm in outward Nature, no Fermentation, Vegetation, or Corruption in any Elementary Things but what is a full Proof and real Effect of this Truth, *viz.,* That Nature can have no Rest but must be in the Strife of Fermentation, Vegetation, and Corruption, constantly doing and undoing, building and destroying, till the *Spirit of Love* has *rectified* all outward Nature and brought it back again into that *glassy Sea* of Unity and Purity in which St. John beheld the Throne of God in the Midst of it. For this *glassy Sea*, which the beloved Apostle was blessed with the Sight of, is the transparent, heavenly Element in which all the Properties and Powers of Nature move and work in the *Unity* and *Purity* of the one Will of God, only known as so many endless Forms of triumphing Light and Love. For the Strife of Properties, of *Thick* against *Thin*, *Hard* against *Soft*, *Hot* against *Cold*, &c., had no Existence till Angels fell, that is till they turned from God to Work with Nature. This is the Original of all the *Strife, Division,* and *Materiality,* in the fallen World.

[Love-1-12] No *Fluid* in this World ferments but because there is some Thickness and Contrariety in it which it would not have. And it ferments only for this Reason, to have a *Unity* and *Clearness* in itself which its Nature wants to have. Now when you see this in any Fluid, you see the Work of all fallen Nature and the *same,* that every Thing else is doing, as well as it can, in its own Way; it is in a restless Working and Strife after a *Unity* and *Purity* which it can neither have nor forbear to seek. And the Reason why all Things are doing thus is this, because all the Elements of this World, before they were brought down into their present State, had their *Birth* and *Existence* in the Unity and Purity of the heavenly *glassy Sea,* and therefore must be always in some Sort of *Strife* and *Tendency* after their first State, and doomed to Disquiet till it is found.

[Love-1-13] This is the Desire of all fallen Nature in this World. It cannot be separated from it but every Part must work in Fermentation, Vegetation, and Corruption, till it is restored to its first Unity and Purity under the Spirit of Love.

[Love-1-14] Every Son of fallen *Adam* is under this *same Necessity* of working and striving after *something* that he neither is nor hath, and for the same Reason, because the Life of Man has lost its first *Unity* and *Purity* and therefore must be in a working Strife till all Contrariety and Impurity is separated from it and it finds its *first State* in God. All evil as well as good Men, all the *Wisdom* and *Folly* of this Life, are equally Proof of this. For the Vanity of wicked Men in their various Ways, and the Labours of good Men in Faith and Hope, &c., proceed from the *same Cause, viz.,* from a *Want* and *Desire* of having and being *something* that they neither are nor have. The Evil seek Wrong and the Good seek Right, but they both are *Seekers*, and for the same Reason, because their present State has not *That* which it wants to have. And this must be the State of human Life and of every Creature that has fallen from its first State or has something in it that it should not have. It must do as the *polluted Fluid* does; it must ferment and work, either *right* or *wrong*, to mend its State. The muddled Wine always works right to the utmost of its Power because it works according to Nature, but if it had an *intelligent free Will* it might work as vainly as Man does; it might continually *thicken* itself, be always stirring up its *own Dregs*, and then it would seek for its Purity, just as well as the Soul of Man seeks its Happiness, in the Lusts of the Flesh, the Lust of the Eyes, and the Pride of Life. All which must of the *same Necessity* fall away from the Heart of Man before it can find its Happiness in God, as the Dregs must *separate* from the Wine before it can have its Perfection and Clearness.

[Love-1-15] *Purification* therefore is the one Thing necessary, and nothing will do in the stead of it. But Man is not purified till every earthly, wrathful, sensual, selfish, partial, self-willing Temper, is taken from him. He is not dying to himself, till he is dying to these Tempers; and he is not alive in God, till he is dead to them. For he wants Purification only because he has these Tempers, and therefore he has not the Purification which he wants till they are all separated from him. It is the Purity and Perfection of the Divine Nature that must be brought again into him; because in that Purity and Perfection he came forth from God, and could have no less, as he was a Child of God, that was to be blessed by a Life in him, and from him. For nothing impure or imperfect in its Will and Working, can have any Union with God. Nor are you to think that these Words, the *Purity* and *Perfection* of God, are too high to be used on this Occasion; for they only mean, that the Will of the Creature, as an *Offspring* of the Divine Will, must *will* and *work* with the Will of God, for then it stands and lives truly and really in the Purity and Perfection of God; and whatever does not thus, is at *Enmity* with God, and cannot have any Union of Life and Happiness with him, and in him.

[Love-1-16] Now, nothing *wills* and *works* with God but the *Spirit of Love*, because nothing else Works in God himself. The Almighty brought forth all Nature for this only End, that boundless Love might have its *Infinity* of Height and Depth to dwell and work in, and all the striving and working Properties of Nature are only to give *Essence* and *Substance*, Life and Strength, to the *invisible hidden Spirit of Love*, that it may come forth into outward Activity and manifest its blessed Powers, that Creatures born in the Strength, and out of the Powers of Nature, might communicate the Spirit of Love and Goodness, give and receive mutual Delight and Joy to and from one another. All below this State of Love is a *Fall* from the one Life of God, and the only Life in which the God of Love can dwell. *Partiality, Self, Mine, Thine, &c.*, are Tempers that can only belong to Creatures that have *lost the Power*, Presence, and Spirit of the *universal Good*. They can have no Place in Heaven, nor can be anywhere but because Heaven is lost. Think not, therefore, that the Spirit of pure, universal Love, which is the one Purity and Perfection of

Heaven, and all heavenly Natures, has been, or can be carried too high, or its absolute Necessity too much asserted. For it admits of no Degrees of higher or lower, and is not in Being till it is absolutely pure and unmixed, no more than a Line can be straight till it is absolutely free from all Crookedness.

[Love-1-17] All the design of Christian Redemption is, to remove every Thing that is *unheavenly, gross, dark, wrathful,* and *disordered,* from every Part of this fallen World. And when you see Earth and Stones, Storms and Tempests, and every kind of Evil, Misery, and Wickedness, you see *that* which Christ came into the World to remove, and not only to give a *new Birth* to fallen Man, but also to deliver all *outward Nature* from its present Vanity and Evil and set it again in its first heavenly State. Now, if you ask, How came all Things into this Evil and Vanity? It is because they have lost the blessed *Spirit of Love,* which alone makes the Happiness and Perfection of every Power of Nature. Look at *Grossness, Coldness, Hardness,* and *Darkness;* they never could have had any Existence, but because the Properties of Nature must appear in *this manner* when the Light of God is no longer dwelling in them.

[Love-1-18] Nature is at first only *spiritual;* it has in itself nothing but the spiritual Properties of the *Desire,* which is the very Being and Ground of Nature. But when these spiritual Properties are not *filled* and *blessed,* and all held in *one Will* by the Light and Love of God ruling in them, then *something* is found in Nature which never should have been found; *viz.,* the Properties of Nature, in a State of visible, palpable *Division* and *Contrariety* to each other. And this new State of the Properties of Nature is the first Beginning and Birth, and Possibility of all that Contrariety that is to be found betwixt *Hot* and *Cold, Hard* and *Soft, Thick* and *Thin,* &c., all which could have had no Existence, till the Properties of Nature lost their first *Unity,* and *Purity* under the Light and Love of God, manifested and working in them. And this is the one true Origin of *all the Materiality* of this earthly *System,* and of every *Struggle* and *Contrariety,* found in material Things. Had the Properties of Nature been kept by the Creature, in their first State, blessed and overcome with the Light and Love of Heaven dwelling and working in them, no *Wrath* or *Contrariety* could ever have been known by any Creature; and had not Wrath and Contrariety entered into the Properties of Nature, nothing *Thick* or *Hard* or *Dark,* &c., could ever have been found or known in *any Place.* Now every Thing that you see and know of the Things of this World, shows you, that *Matter* began only in and from the Change of the *spiritual Properties* of Nature; and that Matter is changed and altered, just as the Light and Purity of Heaven is more or less in it. How comes the *Flint* to be in such a State of hard, dark Compaction? It is because the *Meekness* and *Fluidity* of the Light, and Air, and Water of this World have little or no Existence in it. And therefore, as soon as the Fire has unlocked its hard Compaction and opened in it the Light, and Air, and Water of this World, it becomes transparent Glass, and is brought so much nearer to that first *glassy Sea* in which it once existed. For the *Light,* and Air, and Water, of this World, though all of them in a material State, yet have the most of the first heavenly Nature in them; and as these are more, or less, in all material Things, so are they nearer, or farther from, their first heavenly State. And as Fire is the first Deliverer of the Flint from its hard Compaction, so the last universal Fire must begin the Deliverance of this material *System* and fit every Thing to receive that Spirit of Light and Love, which will bring all Things back again to their first *glassy Sea,* in which the Deity dwelleth, as in his Throne. And thus, as the earthly Fire turns Flint into Glass, so Earth will become Heaven, and the *Contrariety* of *four* divided Elements Will become *one transparent Brightness* of Glory, as soon as the last Fire shall have melted every

Grossness into its first undivided Fluidity, for the Light and Love, and Majesty, of God to be all in all in it. How easy and natural is it to suppose all that is Earth, and Stones, to be dissolved in Water, the Water to be changed into Air, the Air into Aether, and the Aether rarefied into Light? Is there any Thing here impossible to be supposed? And how near a Step is the next, to suppose all this changed or exalted into that *glassy Sea,* which was *everywhere,* before the Angels fell? What now is become of hard, heavy, dead, divisible, corruptible Matter? Is it annihilated? No; And yet nothing of it is left; all that you know of it is gone, and nothing but its *shadowy Idea* will be known in Eternity. Now as this shows you, how Matter can lose all its *material Properties,* and go back to its *first spiritual* State, so it makes it very intelligible to you, how the Sin of Angels, which was their sinful Working in and with the Properties of Nature, could bring them out of their *first Spirituality* into that *Darkness, Grossness,* and *Chaos* out of which God raised this material *System.* See now, Sir, how unreasonably you once told me, that our Doctrine must suppose the *Eternity* of Matter; for throughout the Whole you might easily have seen, that it neither does nor can suppose it, but demonstrates the *Impossibility* of it; shows the true Origin of Matter, that it is no *older* than Sin; could have no Possibility of *beginning* to be, but from Sin, and therefore must entirely *vanish* when Sin is entirely done away.

[Love-1-19] If *Matter,* said you, be not made *out of nothing* then it must be *eternal.* Just as well concluded, as if you had said, If *Snow* and *Hail* and *Ice* are not made out of *nothing,* then they must be *eternal.* And if your Senses did not force you to know, how these things are created out of *something,* and are in themselves only the Properties of Light, and Air, and Water, brought out of their first State into such a Compaction and Creation, as is called Snow, Hail, and Ice, your *rational Philosophy* would stand to its noble Conclusion, that they must be made *out of Nothing.* Now every time you see Snow or Hail or Ice, you see in Truth and Reality the *Creation of Matter,* or how this World came to be of *such a material* Nature as it is. For Earth and Stones, and every other Materiality of this World, came from some *antecedent Properties* of Nature by that *same creating* Power or *Fiat* of God as turns the Properties of *Light,* and *Air,* and *Water,* into the different Materialities of *Snow, Hail,* and *Ice.*

[Love-1-20] The *first Property* of Nature, which is in itself a *constringing, attracting, compressing,* and *coagulating* Power, is that working Power from whence comes all Thickness, Darkness, Coldness, and Hardness; and this is the *Creator* of Snow and Hail and Ice out of *something* that before was only the *Fluidity* of Light, Air, and Moisture. Now this same Property of Nature, directed by the Will of God, was the *Fiat* and *creating Power* which, on the first Day of this World, compacted, coagulated, or created the *wrathful Properties* of fallen Nature in the Angelic Kingdom into such a new State as to become *Earth* and *Stones* and *Water and a visible Heaven.* And the new State of the created Heaven and Earth and Stones and Water, *&c.,* came forth by the *Fiat* of God, or the Working of the first Property of Nature, from the Properties of fallen Nature; just as Snow and Ice and Hail, come forth by the same *Fiat* from the Properties of Light, Air, and Water. And the *created Materiality* of Heaven, Earth, Stones, and Water, have *no more Eternity* in them, than there is in Snow or Hail or Ice, but are only held for a time in their compacted or created State, by the same first astringing Property of Nature, which for *a time* holds Snow and Hail and Ice in their compacted State.

[Love-1-21] Now here you see with the utmost Certainty that all the *Matter* or *Materiality* of this World is the Effect of Sin, and could have its Beginning from nothing else. For as Thickness,

Hardness, and Darkness (which is the Essence of Matter) is the Effect of the wrathful predominant Power of the *first Property* of Nature, and as no Property of Nature can be predominant, or known as it is in itself, till Nature is *fallen* from its harmonious Unity under the *Light and Love* of God dwelling in it, so you have the utmost Certainty, that where Matter, or which is the same Thing, where *Thickness, Darkness, Hardness, &c.,* are found, there the Will of the Creature has *turned* from God and opened a disorderly Working of Nature without God.

[Love-1-22] Therefore as sure as the *Materiality* of this World standeth in the *predominant Power* of the first attracting, astringing Property of Nature, or in other Words, is a *Thickness, Darkness, Hardness, &c.,* so sure is it that all the *Matter* of this World has its *Beginning* from Sin and must have its *End* as soon as the Properties of Nature are again restored to their first Unity and blessed Harmony under the Light and Spirit of God.

[Love-1-23] It is no Objection to all this, that Almighty God must be owned to be the true Creator of the Materiality of this World. For God only brought or created it into this Materiality out of the *fallen sinful* Properties of Nature, and in order to *stop* their sinful Working, and to put them into a State of Recovery. He created the confused Chaos of the *darkened, divided, contrary* Properties of spiritual Nature into a further, *darker, harder Coagulation* and *Division*, that so the fallen Angels might thereby *lose* all Power over them, and that this *new Materiality* might become a Theatre of Redemption and stand *its Time* under the Dominion of the *Lamb of God* till all the *Wrath* and *Grossness* and *Darkness*, born of the Sin of the Angels, was fitted to return to its first heavenly Purity.

[Love-1-24] And thus, though God is the Creator of the Materiality of this World, yet seeing he created it out of that *Wrath, Division*, and *Darkness* which Sin had opened in Nature, this Truth stands firm, that Sin alone is the *Father*, first *Cause*, and *Beginner* of all the Materiality of this World; and that when Sin is removed from Nature all its Materiality must vanish with it. For when the Properties of Nature are again in the Unity of the *one Will* of Light and Love, *then Hot* and *Cold, Thick* and *Thin, Dark* and *Hard*, with every Property of Matter, must give up all their Distinction, and all the divided Elements of this World *lose* all their *Materiality* and *Division* in that first heavenly Spirituality of a *glassy Sea* from whence they fell.

[Love-1-25] Now as all the whole Nature of *Matter*, its Grossness, Darkness, and Hardness, is owing to the *unequal, predominant* Working of the first Property of Nature which is an *attracting, astringing*, and *compressing* Desire; so every *spiritual* Evil, every wicked Working and disorderly State of any intelligent Being is all owing to the *same disorderly, predominant* Power of the first Property of Nature, doing all that *inwardly* in the Spirit of the Creature, which it does in an outward Grossness, Darkness, and Hardness. Thus, when the *Desire* (the first Property of Nature) in any intelligent Creature, leaves the *Unity* and *Universality* of the Spirit of Love and *contracts* or *shuts* up itself in an *own Will, own Love*, and *Self-seeking*, then it does *all that* inwardly and spiritually in the Soul, which it does in outward Grossness, Hardness, and Darkness. And had not *own Will, own Love*, and *Self-seeking* come into the Spirit of the Creature, it never could have found or felt any *outward* Contrariety, Darkness or Hardness: For no Creature can have any *other outward* Nature but that which is in the same State with its inward Spirit, and belongs to it as its own *natural Growth*.

[Love-1-26] Modern *Metaphysics* has no Knowledge of the Ground and Nature either of *Spirit* or *Body*, but supposes them not only without *any natural* Relation, but *essentially* contrary to one another, and only held together in a *forced* Conjunction by the *arbitrary Will* of God. Nay, if you were to say that God first creates a Soul *out of nothing*, and when that is done, then takes an *understanding Faculty* and puts it into it, after that adds a *Will* and then a *Memory*, all is independently made, as when a Tailor first makes the Body of a Coat and then adds Sleeves or Pockets to it, were you to say This, the Schools of *Descartes*, *Malebranche*, or *Locke* could have nothing to say against it. And the Thing is unavoidable, for all these Philosophers were so far from knowing the *Ground* of Nature, how it is a *Birth* from God, and all Creatures a *Birth* from Nature, through the working Will of God in and by the Powers of Nature, as they were so far from knowing this, as to hold a Creation *out of nothing*, so they were necessarily *excluded* from every fundamental Truth concerning the Origin either of Body or Spirit and their true Relation to one another. For a Creation *out of nothing* leaves no room for accounting why any Thing is as it is.— Now every wise Man is supposed to have Respect to Nature in every Thing that he would have joined together; he cannot suppose his Work to succeed unless this be done. But to suppose God to create Man with a Body and Soul, not only not *naturally* related but naturally *impossible* to be united by any Powers in either of them, is to suppose God acting and creating Man into an *unnatural State*, which yet he could not do, unless there was such a Thing as Nature *antecedent* to the Creation of Man. And how can Nature be, or have any Thing but what it is and has from God? Therefore to suppose God to bring any Creature into an unnatural State is to suppose him acting *contrary* to himself and to that Nature which is from him.

[Love-1-27] Yet all the Metaphysics of the *Schools* does this. It supposes God to bring a Soul and a Body together which have the *utmost natural* Contrariety to each other and can only affect or act upon one another by an *arbitrary Will* of God, willing that Body and Soul, held together by *Force*, should *seem* to do that to one another which they have no *natural* or *possible* Power to do. But the true Philosophy of this Matter, known only to the Soul, that by a new Birth from above has found its first State in and from God is this: *Namely*, that Nature is a Birth or Manifestation of the triune invisible Deity. And as it could only come into Existence as a *Birth* from God, so every Creature or beginning Thing can only come forth as a *Birth* from and out of Nature by the Will of God, willing it to come forth in such a Birth. And no Creature can have, or be, any Thing, but by and according to the working Powers of Nature; and therefore, strictly speaking, no Creature can be, or be put into an *unnatural* State. It may indeed *lose* or *fall* from its *natural Perfection* by the wrong Use or Working of its Will; but then its *fallen* State is the *natural Effect* of the wrong Use of its Will, and so it only has *that* which is *natural* to it. The Truth of the Matter is this: There neither is, nor can be, any Thing, nor any Effect in the whole Universe of Things but by the *Way of Birth*. For as the *working Will* is the first Cause or Beginner of every Thing, so nothing can proceed *further* than as it is *driven* by the Will and is a *Birth of* it. And therefore nothing can be in any Thing but what is *natural* to its *own working* Will and the true *Effect* of it. Every Thing that is outward in any Being is only *a Birth* of its own Spirit, and therefore all Body, whether it be heavenly or earthly or hellish, has its whole *Nature* and *Condition* from its *own* inward Spirit, and no Spirit can have a Body of any *other Properties* but such as are *natural* to it as being its *own true outward* State. For Body and Spirit are not two *separate, independent* Things, but are *necessary* to each other, and are only the *inward* and *outward* conditions of *one* and the *same Being*.

[Love-1-28] Every *creaturely* Spirit must have its *own Body* and cannot be without it, for its Body is *that* which makes it *manifest* to itself. It cannot be said to exist as a *Creature* till in a Body, because it can have no *Sensibility* of itself, nor feel nor find either that it is, or what it is, but in and by its own Body. Its Body is its first Knowledge of its *Something* and *Somewhere*.

[Love-1-29] And now, Sir, if you ask why I have gone into this Detail of the *Origin* and *Nature* of Body and Spirit, when my Subject was only concerning the Spirit of Love, it is to show you, that *Grossness, Darkness, Contrariety, Disquiet,* and *Fermentation* must be the State of the Body and Spirit till they are both made *pure* and *luminous* by the Light and Love of Heaven manifested in them. All Darkness, Grossness, and Contrariety must be removed from the Body before it can belong to Heaven, or be united with it; but these Qualities must be in the Body till the Soul is totally dead to *Self, Partiality,* and *Contrariety,* and breathes only the Spirit of universal Love, because the State of the Body has nothing of *its own,* or from itself, but is solely the *outward Manifestation* of nothing else but that which is *inwardly in the Soul.* Every Animal of this World has nothing in its outward Form or Shape, every Spirit, whether heavenly or hellish, has nothing in the Nature and State of its Body, but that which is the Form and Growth of its own *inward Spirit.* As no Number can be any Thing else but that which the *Unities* contained in it make it to be, so no *Body* of any Creature can be any Thing else but the Coagulation, or S*um total,* of those Properties of Nature that are coagulated in it. And when the Properties of Nature are formed into the band of a *creaturely Union,* then is its Body brought forth, whether the Spirit of the Creature be earthly, heavenly, or hellish.

[Love-1-30] Nature, or the *first Properties* of Life, are in a State of the highest Contrariety, and the highest Want of *something* which they have not. This is their whole Nature and they have nothing else in them. And this is their true Ground and Fitness to become a Life of triumphing Joy and Happiness, *viz.,* when united in the Possession of that which they seek for in their Contrariety. And if Life, in its first Root, was not this Depth of Strife, this Strength of Hunger, and Sensibility of Want, the Fullness of heavenly Joy could not be manifested in it.

[Love-1-31] You are not a Stranger to the Mystery of the *Seven Properties* of Nature which we have often spoken of; and therefore I shall shorten the Matter, and only say so much of them as may be of Service to our present Subject.

[Love-1-32] Nature, whether eternal or temporal, is *That* which comes not into Being for its own Self or to be *That* which it is in itself, but for the Sake of *Something* that it is not, and has not. And this is the Reason why Nature is only a *Desire*; it is because it is for the Sake of *something else;* and is also the Reason why Nature in itself is only a *Torment,* because it is only a strong Desire, and cannot help itself to that which it wants, but is always working against itself.

[Love-1-33] Now a Desire that cannot be *stopped,* nor get That which it would have, has a *threefold* Contrariety, or Working in it, which you may thus conceive as follows: The first and *peculiar* Property, or the *one only* Will of the Desire, as such, is to *have* That which it has not; and all it can do toward *having* it is to act as if it were *seizing* it; and this is it which makes the Desire to be *a magic Compressing, Inclosing,* or *Astringing,* because that is all that it can do toward *Seizing* of that which it would have. But the Desire cannot thus magically *astringe, compress,* or strive to inclose, without *Drawing* and *Attracting*: But Drawing is *Motion,* which is the highest Contrariety and Resistance to *compressing* or *holding together*. And thus the Desire, in its magical Working, sets out with *two contrary* Properties, inseparable from one another and equal in Strength; for the Motion has no Strength but as it is the *Drawing* of the Desire; and the Desire only *draws* in the *same Degree* as it wills to *compress* and *astringe*; and therefore the Desire, as *astringing*, always begets a *Resistance* equal to itself. Now from this great and equally strong Contrariety of the *two first Properties* of the Desire, magically pulling, as I may say, two contrary Ways, there arises as a necessary Birth from both of them, a *third Property,* which is emphatically called a *Wheel* or *whirling Anguish* of Life. For a Thing that can go neither inward nor outward, and yet must *be* and *move* under the equal Power of both of them, must *whirl* or *turn round*; it has no Possibility of doing any Thing else or of ceasing to do that. And that this *whirling Contrariety* of these inseparable Properties is the *great Anguish* of Life and may properly be called the *Hell of Nature*; and every lesser Torment which any Man finds in this mixed World, has all its Existence and Power from the Working of these *three* Properties: For Life can find no troublesome Motions, or Sensibility of Distress, but so far as it comes under their Power, and enters into their whirling Wheel.

[Love-1-34] Now here you may observe, that as this *whirling* Anguish of Life is a *third State,* necessarily arising from the Contrariety of the *two first* Properties of the Desire, so in this material System, every *whirling* or *orbicular* Motion of any Body is solely the Effect or Product of the Contrariety of *these two* first Properties. For no material Thing can whirl or move round, till it is under the Power of these *two Properties*; that is, till it can neither go inwards nor outwards, and yet is obliged to *move*, just as the whirling Anguish of the Desire then begins when it can neither go inwards nor outwards and yet must be in *Motion*.

[Love-1-35] And this may be again another strict Demonstration to you, that all the *Matter* of this World is from *spiritual Properties*, since all its Workings and Effects are according to them: For if Matter does nothing but according to them, it can be nothing but what it is, and has from them.

[Love-1-36] Here also, that is, in these *three Properties* of the Desire, you see the Ground and Reason of the *three* great Laws of *Matter* and *Motion,* lately discovered, and so much celebrated, and need no more to be told, that the illustrious Sir *Isaac* plowed with *Behmen's* Heifer, when he brought forth the Discovery of them. In the mathematical System of this great Philosopher these three Properties, *Attraction*, equal *Resistance*, and the *orbicular Motion* of the Planets as the effect of them, *&c.*, are only treated of as *Facts* and *Appearances*, whose Ground is not pretended to be known. But in our *Behmen*, the illuminated Instrument of God, their *Birth* and *Power* in Eternity are opened; their eternal Beginning is shown, and *how* and *why* all Worlds, and every Life of every Creature, whether it be heavenly, earthly, or hellish, must be in them, and from them, and can have no Nature either spiritual or material, no kind of Happiness or Misery, but according to the working Power and State of these Properties.

[Love-1-37] All outward Nature, all inward Life, is what it is, and works as it works, from this unceasing, powerful *Attraction, Resistance*, and *Whirling*.

[Love-1-38] Every Madness and Folly of Life is their immediate Work and every good Spirit of Wisdom and Love has all its Strength and Activity from them. They equally support Darkness and Light: The one could have no Powers of Thickness and Coldness, the other no Powers of Warmth, Brightness, and Activity but by and through these three Properties acting in a different State. Not a Particle of Matter stirs, rises, or falls, separates from or unites with any other, but under their Power. Not a Thought of the Mind, either of Love or Hatred, of Joy or Trouble, of Envy or Wrath, of Pride and Covetousness, can rise in the Spirit of any Creature, but as these Properties act and stir in it.

[Love-1-39] The next and following Properties, *viz.*, the fourth, called *Fire*; the fifth, called the Form of *Light and Love*, and the sixth, *Sound*, or *Understanding*, only declare the *gradual Effects* of the Entrance of the Deity into the three first Properties of Nature, changing, or bringing their strong wrathful *Attraction, Resistance,* and *Whirling*, into a Life and State of triumphing Joy, and Fullness of Satisfaction; which State of Peace and Joy in one another is called the *Seventh Property*, or State of Nature. And this is what *Behmen* means by his *Ternarius Sanctus*, which he so often speaks of as the only Place from whence he received all that he said and wrote: He means by it the holy Manifestation of the Triune God in the *seven Properties* of Nature, or Kingdom of Heaven. And from this Manifestation of God in the seven Properties of Nature, or Kingdom of Heaven, he most wonderfully opens, and accounts for all that was done in the *six first working Days* of the Creation, showing how every one of the six active Properties had its *peculiar* Day's Work, till the whole ended or *rested* in the sanctified, *paradisiacal* Sabbath of the *seventh Day*, just as Nature doth in its *seventh Property*.

[Love-1-40] And now, Sir, you may see in the greatest Clearness how every Thing in this World, every Thing in the Soul and Body of Man, absolutely requires the *one Redemption* of the Gospel. There is but *one Nature* in all created Things, whether spiritual or material; they all stand and work upon the same Ground, *viz.*, the *three first Properties* of Nature. That only which can illuminate the Soul, that alone can give *Brightness* and *Purity* to the Body. For there is no Grossness, Darkness, and Contrariety in the Body, but what strictly proceeds from the *same* Cause that makes Selfishness, Wrath, Envy, and Torment in the Soul; it is but one and the same State and Working of the same three first Properties of Nature. All Evil, whether natural or moral, whether of Body or Spirit, is the sole Effect of the *Wrath* and *Disorder* of the Spirits of Nature working in and by themselves. And all the Good, Perfection, and Purity of every Thing, whether spiritual or material, whether it be the Body or Spirit of Man or Angel, is solely from the Power and Presence of the supernatural Deity *dwelling* and *working* in the Properties of Nature. For the Properties of Nature are in themselves nothing else but a mere *Hunger, Want, Strife,* and *Contrariety*, till the Fullness and Riches of the Deity entering into them unites them all in *one Will* and *one Possession* of Light and harmonious Love; which is the *one Redemption* of the Gospel, and the one Reason why nothing else but the *Heart*, or *Son*, or *Light* of God, can purify Nature and Creature from all the Evil they are fallen into.

[Love-1-41] For nothing can possibly deliver the Soul from its *selfish* Nature and *earthly* Passions but that *one Power* that can deliver *Matter* from its present material Properties and turn Earth into Heaven: And that for this plain Reason, because Soul and Body, outward Nature and inward Life, have but one and the same Evil in them, and from one and the same Cause.

[Love-1-42] The *Deist*, therefore, who looks for Life and Salvation through the Use of his Reason, acts contrary to the whole Nature of every Thing that he sees and knows of himself and of the Nature and State of this World. For from one End of it to the other, all its material State, all its gross divided Elements, declare that they are what they are, because the Light and Love of Heaven is not working and manifest in them, and that nothing can take Darkness, Materiality, Rage, Storms, and Tempests from them, but that same heavenly Light and Love which was made Flesh to redeem the fallen Humanity first, and after that the whole material System.

[Love-1-43] Can the Deist with his Reason bring the Light of this World into the Eyes of his Body? If not, how comes it to be less absurd, or more possible, for Reason to bring heavenly Light into the Soul? Can Reason hinder the Body from being heavy, or remove Thickness and Darkness from Flesh and Blood? Yet nothing less than such a Power can possibly help the Soul out of its fallen and earthly State. For the Grossness of Flesh and Blood is the *natural State* of the fallen Soul; and therefore nothing can purify the Soul, or raise it out of its earthly, corrupt State, but that which hath all Power over all that, that is *earthy* and *material* in Nature.

[Love-1-44] To pretend, therefore, that Reason may have sufficient Power to remove all hellish Depravity and earthly Lusts from the Soul, whilst it has not the least Power over *Sweet* or *Sour* in any one Particle of Matter in the Body, is as highly absurd, as if a Man should pretend that he has a full Power to alter the inward, invisible, vegetable Life of a Plant, but none at all over its outward State, Colour, Leaves, or Fruit. The *Deist* therefore, and not the Christian, stands in need of continual Miracles to make good his Doctrine. For Reason can have no Pretence to amend or alter the Life of the Soul, but so far as it can show that it has Power to amend and alter the Nature and State of the Body.

[Love-1-45] The unbelieving *Jews* said of our Lord, "How can this Man forgive Sins?" Christ showed them *how* by appealing to that Power which they saw he had over the Body: "Whether," says he, "is it easier to say, Thy Sins are forgiven thee, or to say, Arise, take up thy Bed, and walk?" But the Delusion of the unbelieving Deist is greater than that of the *Jew*. For the Deist sees, that his Reason has no Power over his Body, can remove no Disease, Blindness, Deafness, or Lameness, from it, and yet will pretend to have Power enough from his Reason to help the Soul out of all its Evil; not knowing that Body and Soul go hand in hand, and are nothing else but the inward and outward State of *one and the same* Life; and that therefore he only, who can say to the dead Body of *Lazarus*, "Come forth," can say to the Soul, "Be thou clean." The *Deist* therefore, if he pleases, may style himself a natural or a moral Philosopher, but with no more Truth than he can call himself a *Healer* of all the Maladies of the Body. And for a Man to think himself a moral Philosopher, because he has made a choice Collection of Syllogisms, in order to quicken and revive a Divine Goodness in the Soul, or that no Redeemer need come from Heaven, because human Reason, when truly left to itself, has great Skill in chopping of Logic; may justly be deemed such an Ignorance of the Nature of Things as is seldom found in the Transactions of illiterate and vulgar Life. But this by the by.

[Love-1-46] To return to our chief subject: The Sum of all that has been said is this: All Evil, be it what it will, all Misery of every kind, is in its Birth, Working and Extent, nothing else but Nature left to *itself*, and under the divided Workings of its own *Hunger, Wrath*, and *Contrariety*; and therefore no Possibility for the natural, earthly Man to escape eternal Hunger, Wrath, and Contrariety, but solely in the Way as the Gospel teacheth, by denying and dying to Self. On the other hand, all the Goodness and Perfection, all the Happiness, Glory, and Joy that any intelligent, Divine Creature can be possessed of, is, and can be, from nothing else, but the *invisible uncreated Light and Spirit* of God manifesting itself in the Properties of the creaturely Life, *filling, blessing*, and *uniting* them all in *one Love* and Joy of Life. And thus again: no Possibility of Man's attaining to any heavenly Perfection and Happiness, but only in the Way of the Gospel, by the *Union* of the Divine and human Nature, by Man's being born again from above of the *Word* and *Spirit* of God. There is no Possibility of any other Way, because there is nothing that can possibly change the first Properties of Life into an heavenly State, but the Presence, and working Power, of the Deity united with, and working in them. And therefore the "Word was made Flesh," and must of all Necessity be made Flesh, if Man is to have a heavenly Nature. Now as all Evil, Sin, and Misery, have no Beginning, nor Power of Working, but in the Manifestation of Nature in its *divided, contrary* Properties; so it is certain that Man has nothing to turn to, seek or aspire after, but the lost *Spirit of Love*. And therefore it is, that God only can be his Redeemer, because God only is Love; and Love can be nowhere else but in God, and where God dwelleth and worketh.

[Love-1-47] Now the Difficulty which you find in attaining to this Purity, and Universality of the Spirit of Love is because you seek for it, as I once told you, in the Way of reasoning: You would be possessed of it only from a *rational* Conviction of the Fitness and Amiableness of it. And as this clear Idea does not put you immediately into the real Possession of it, your Reason begins to waver, and suggests to you, that it may be only a *fine Notion* that has no Ground but in the Power of the Imagination. But this, Sir, is all your own Error, and as contrary to Nature, as if you would have your Eyes do That which only your Hands or Feet can do for you. The *Spirit of Love* is a Spirit of *Nature* and *Life*; and all the Operations of Nature and Life are according to the working Powers of Nature; and every Growth and Degree of Life can only arise in its *own* Time and Place from its *proper* Cause, and as the genuine Effect of it. Nature and Life do nothing by Chance or accidentally, but every Thing in one uniform Way. *Fire, Air,* and *Light,* do not proceed sometimes from one Thing, and sometimes from another; but wherever they are, they are always born in the same Manner, and from the same Working in the Properties of Nature. So in like Manner, Love is an *immutable Birth*, always proceeding from the *same Cause*, and cannot be in Existence till its own true Parents have brought it forth.

[Love-1-48] How unreasonable would it be to begin to doubt whether *Strength* and *Health* of Body were real Things, or possible to be had, because you could not by the Power of your Reason take Possession of them? Yet this is as well as to suspect the Purity and Perfection of Love to be only a *Notion*, because your Reason cannot bring forth its Birth in your Soul. For Reason has no more Power of altering the *Life* and *Properties* of the Soul, than of altering the Life and Properties of the Body. That, and That only, can cast Devils and evil Spirits out of the Soul, that can say to the Storm, *Be still*, and to the Leper, *Be thou clean*.

[Love-1-49] The Birth of Love is a *Form* or *State* of Life, and has its *fixed Place* in the *fifth* Form of Nature. The three first Properties or Forms of Nature are the *Ground* or *Band* of Life, that is in itself only an extreme Hunger, Want, Strife, and Contrariety. And they are in this State, that they may become a proper Fuel for the *fourth* Form of Nature, *viz.,* the *Fire*, to be kindled in them. You will perhaps say, "What is this *Fire*? What is its *Nature*? And how is it kindled? And *how* is it that the Hunger and anguishing State of the Properties, are a Fitness to be a *Fuel* of this Fire?" It may be answered, This Hunger and Anguish of Nature, in its first Forms, is its Fitness to be changed into a Life of Light, Joy, and Happiness: And that for this Reason, because it is in this Hunger and Anguish only because God is *not in it.* For as Nature comes from God, and for this only End, that the Deity may manifest Heaven in it, it must stand in an Hunger and anguishing State till the Deity is manifested in it. And therefore its Hunger and Anguish are its *true Fitness* to be changed into a better State, and this is its *Fitness* for the Birth of the Fire: For the Fire means nothing, and is nothing else, but *That* which changes them into a *better State.* Not as if Fire was a fourth, distinct Thing that comes into them from without, but is only a fourth *State*, or Condition into which the same Properties are brought.

[Love-1-50] The Fire then is *that* which changes the Properties into a *new* and *heavenly* State: Therefore the Fire does two things; it alters the State of Nature and brings Heaven into it, and therefore it must Work from a two-fold Power; the *Deity* and *Nature* must both be in it. It must have some Strength from Nature, or it could not work in Nature. It must have some Strength from the Deity or it could not *overcome* and *change* Nature into a Divine Life. Now all this is only to show you, that the Fire can only be kindled by the *Entrance* of the Deity, or *supernatural* God, into a *Conjunction* or *Union* with Nature. And this Conjunction of the Deity and Nature maketh, or bringeth forth, that *State* or Form of Life, which is called and truly is, *Fire: First*, Because it does *that* in the spiritual Properties of Nature, which Fire doth in the Properties of material Nature; and *Secondly*, Because it is that alone, from which every Fire in this World, whether in the Life of animal or vegetable or inanimate Matter, has its Source and Power and Possibility of Burning. The Fire of this World overcomes its Fuel, breaks its Nature, alters its State and changes it into Flame and Light. But why does it do this? Whence has it this Nature and Power? It is because it is a *true Outbirth* of the *eternal Fire,* which overcomes the Darkness, Wrath, and Contrariety of Nature, and changes all its Properties into a Life of Light, Joy, and Glory. Not a Spark of Fire could be kindled in this World, nor a Ray of Light come from any material Fire, but because material Nature is, in itself, nothing else but the *very Properties* of eternal Nature, standing for a Time in a *material State* or Condition; and therefore they must work in Time as they do in Eternity; and consequently there must be *Fire* in this World, it must have the *same Birth* and do the *same Work* in its *material Way*, which the eternal Fire hath, and doth in spiritual Nature. And this is the true Ground and Reason why every Thing in this World is delivered as far as it can be from its earthly Impurity, and brought into its *highest* State of Existence, only by Fire; it is because the eternal Fire is the *Purifier* of eternal Nature and the *Opener* of every Perfection, Light, and Glory in it. And if you ask why the eternal Fire is the *Purifier* of eternal Nature, the Reason is plain; it is because the eternal Fire has its *Birth* and *Nature* and Power from the Entrance of the pure, supernatural Deity into the Properties of Nature, which Properties must change their State, and be what they were not before, as soon as the Deity *entereth* into them. Their *Darkness*, *Wrath*, and *Contrariety,* is driven out of them, and they work and give forth only a Life and Strength of Light, and Joy, and Glory. And this two-fold Operation, *viz.,* on one hand taking from Nature its *wrathful* Workings, and on the other hand opening a glorious Manifestation of the Deity in them, is the *whole Nature* and *Form* of the Fire, and is the Reason why from Eternity to Eternity it is and must be the *Purifier* of eternal Nature; namely, as from Eternity to Eternity changing Nature into a Kingdom of Heaven. Now every Fire in this World does, and must do, the same Thing in its low Way, to the utmost of its Power, and can do nothing else. Kindle Fire where, or in what you will, it acts only as from and by the Power of this *eternal purifying Fire*; and therefore it breaks and consumes the Grossness of every Thing, and makes all that is pure and spirituous to come forth out of it; and therefore

Purification is its one only Work through all material Nature, because it is a real *Out-birth* of that *eternal Fire* which purifies eternal Nature, and changes it into a mere Heaven of Glory.

[Love-1-51] The eternal Fire is called a *fourth Form,* or State of Nature; because it cannot exist but from the first Three and hath its Work in the *fourth Place* in the Midst of the seven Forms, changing the three first into the three last Forms of Nature, that is, changing them from their natural into a heavenly State. So that, strictly speaking, there are but three Forms of Nature in answerableness to the threefold Working of the Triune Deity. For the three last are not three new or different Properties, but are only the three first brought into a new State by the *Entrance* of the Triune Deity into Conjunction with them. Which Entrance of the supernatural Deity into them is the *consuming* of all that is bad in them, and turning all their Strength into a working Life of Light, Joy, and heavenly Glory; and therefore has the justest Title to be called *Fire*, as having no other Nature and Operation in it but the known Nature of Fire, and also as being *That* from which every Fire in this World has all its Nature and Power of doing as it doth.

[Love-1-52] You once, as I remember, objected to my speaking so much in the *Appeal, &c.*, of the *Fire of Life,* as thinking it too gross an Expression to be taken in its *literal* Meaning, when mention is made of the eternal Fire, or the *Fire* in animal Life. But, Sir, Fire has but *one Nature* through the whole Universe of Things, and material Fire has not more or less of the Nature of Fire in it, than that which is in eternal Nature; because it has nothing, works nothing, but what it has, and works from thence. How easy was it for you to have seen, that the Fire of the Soul and the Fire of the Body had but *one Nature*? How else could they *unite* in their Heat? How easy also to have seen that the Fire of animal Life was the same Fire that burns in the Kitchen? How else could the Kitchen Fire be serviceable to animal Life? What Good could it do you to come to a Fire of Wood where you wanted to have the Heat of your *own Life* increased? In animal Life the Fire is kindled and preserved in such a *Degree,* and in such *Circumstances,* as to be *Life,* and the *Preservation* of Life; and this is its Difference from Fires kindled in Wood and burning it to Ashes. It is the *same Fire*, only in a *different* State, that *keeps up* Life and *consumes* Wood; and has no other Nature in the Wood than in the Animal. Just as in Water that has only so much Fire in it as to make it warm, and Water that is by Fire made boiling hot, the same Nature and Power of Fire is in both, but only in a different State. Now will you say, that Fire is not to be *literally* understood, when it only makes Water to be warm, because it is not *red* and *flaming* as you see it in a burning Coal? Yet this would be as well as to say, that Fire is not *literally* to be understood in the animal Life, because it is so different from that Fire which you see burning in a Piece of Wood. And thus, Sir, there is no Foundation for any Objection to all that has been said of Fire in the *Appeal, &c.* It is one and the same great Power of God in the spiritual and material World; it is the Cause of every Life and the Opener of every Power of Nature; and its one great Work through all Nature and Creature, animate and inanimate, is *Purification* and *Exaltation*; it can do nothing else, and that for this plain Reason, because its Birth is from the Entrance of the pure Deity into Nature, and therefore must in its various State and Degrees be only doing *that* which the *Entrance* of the Deity into Nature does. It must bring every natural Thing into its *highest State*. But to go back now to the *Spirit of Love* and show you the *Time* and *Place* of its Birth before which it can have no Existence in your Soul, do what you will to have it.

[Love-1-53] The *Fire*, you see, is the first *Overcomer* of the hungry, wrathful, self-tormenting State of the Properties of Nature; and it only overcomes them, because it is the *Entrance* of the pure Deity into them; and therefore That which overcomes them is the *Light* of the Deity. And this is the true Ground and Reason why every right-kindled Fire must give forth Light, and cannot do otherwise. It is because the eternal Fire is only the Effect or Operation of the *supernatural Light* of the Deity *entering* into Nature; and therefore Fire must give forth Light, because it is itself only a *Power* of the Light, and Light can be nowhere in Nature but as a *fifth Form* or *State* of Nature, brought forth by the Fire. And as Light thus brought forth is *the first State* that is *lovely* and *delightful* in Nature, so the Spirit of Love has only its Birth *in the Light* of Life, and can be nowhere else. For the Properties of Life have no *common Good*, nothing to rejoice in, till the Light is found; and therefore no possible Beginning of the Spirit of Love till then.

[Love-1-54] The Shock that is given to the three first Properties of Nature by the amazing Light of the Deity breaking in upon them, is the *Operation* of the Fire, that consumes, or takes away, the wrathful Strength and Contrariety of the Properties, and forces each of them to shrink, as it were, away from itself, and come under the Power of this new-risen Light. Here all Strife of Enmity and wrathful Contrariety in the Properties must cease, because all are united in the *Love of the Light*, and all equally helping one another to a higher Enjoyment and Delight in it. They are all one Triune Will, all doing the same Thing, *viz.*, all rejoicing in the one Love of the Light. And here it is, in this delightful Unity of Operation, that the *Spirit of Love* is born, in the *fifth Property* or Light of Life; and cannot possibly rise up in any Creature till the Properties of its Life are brought into this *fifth State*, thus changed and exalted into a new Sensibility of Life. Let me give you this Similitude of the Matter: Fancy to yourself a Man shut up in a deep Cave underground, without ever having seen a Ray of the Light, his Body all over tortured with Pain, his Mind distracted with Rage, himself whirling and working with the utmost Fury and Madness, he knows not what; and then you have an Image of the first Properties of Life as they are in themselves before the Fire had done its Work in them.

[Love-1-55] Fancy this Man suddenly struck, or all surrounded, with such a Glare of Light as in the Twinkling of an Eye stopped or struck dead, every Working of every Pain and Rage, both in his Body and Mind; and then you have an Image of the *Operation* of the Fire, and what it does to the first Properties of Nature. Now as soon as the first Terror of the Light has had its fiery Operation, and struck nothing dead but every working Sensibility of Distress, fancy this Man, as you now well may, in the sweetest Peace of Mind and bodily Sensations, blessed in a new Region of Light, giving Joy to his Mind, and Gratification to every Sense; and then the Transports, the Overflowings of Love and Delight in this new State may give you an Image how the *Spirit of Love* is, and must be born, when Fire and Light have overcome and changed the State of the first Properties of Nature; and never *till then,* can have any Existence in any Creature, nor proceed from any other Cause. Thus, Sir, you may sufficiently see, how vainly you attempt to possess yourself of the Spirit of Love by the Power of your Reason; and also what a Vanity of all Vanities there is in the Religion of the Deists, who will have no other Perfection, or Divine Life, but what they can have from their Reason: as great a Contradiction to Nature, as if they would have no Life or Strength of Body, but that which can be had from their Faculty of Reasoning. For Reason can no more alter or exalt any *one Property* of Life in the Soul, and bring it into its *perfect State,* than it can add one Cubit to the Stature of the Body. The Perfection of every Life is no way possibly to be had, but as every Flower comes to its Perfection, *viz.*, from its own Seed and Root and the various Degrees of Transmutation which must be gone through before the Flower is found: It is strictly thus with the Perfection of the Soul: All its Properties of Life must have their true natural Birth and Growth from one another. The first, as its *Seed* and Root, must have their natural change into an higher State; must, like the Seed of the Flower, pass through Death into Life and be blessed with the Fire and Light and Spirit of Heaven, in their Passage to it; just as the Seed passes through Death into Life, blessed by the Fire, and Light, and Air of this World, till it reaches its last Perfection, and becomes a beautiful sweet-smelling Flower. And to think that the Soul can attain its Perfection any other Way, than by the *Change* and *Exaltation* of its first Properties of Life, just as the Seed has its first Properties *changed* and *exalted* till it comes to have its Flower, is a total Ignorance of the Nature of Things. For as whatever dies cannot have a Death *particular* to itself, but the same Death in the same Way, and for the same Reasons, that any other Creature, whether Animal or vegetable, ever did or can die; so every Life and Degree of Life, must come into its State and Condition of Life in the same Way, and for the same Reasons as Life, and the Perfection of Life, comes into every other living Creature, whether in Heaven or on Earth. Therefore the Deists' Religion or Reason, which is to raise the Soul to its true Perfection, is so far from being the Religion of Nature, that it is quite unnatural and declared to be so by every Working in Nature. For since Reason can neither give Life nor Death to any one Thing in Nature, but every Thing lives, or dies, according to the Working of its own Properties, every Thing, dead and alive, gives forth a Demonstration, that Nature asks no Counsel of Reason, nor stays to be directed by it. Hold it therefore for a certain Truth, that you can have no Good come into your Soul, but only by the *one Way* of a Birth from above, from the *Entrance of the Deity* into the Properties of your own soulish Life. Nature must be set right, its Properties must enter into the Process of a new Birth, it must work to the Production of Light, before the Spirit of Love can have a Birth in it. For Love is Delight, and Delight cannot arise in any Creature till its Nature is in a delightful State, or is possessed of that in which it must rejoice. And this is the Reason why God must become Man; it is because a Birth of the Deity must be found in the Soul, giving to Nature all that it wants, or the Soul can never find itself in a delightful State and only Working with the *Spirit of Love*. For whilst the Soul has only its *natural Life*, it can only be in such a State, as Nature, without God, is in, *viz.*, a mere *Hunger, Want, Contrariety*, and *Strife* for it knows not what. Hence is all that Variety of *blind, restless, contrary* Passions, which govern and torment the Life of fallen Man. It is because all the Properties of Nature must Work in *Blindness,* and be doing *they know not what,* till the *Light* of God is found in them. Hence also it is, that That which is called the *Wisdom*, the *Honour*, the *Honesty*, and the *Religion* of the natural Man, often does as much Hurt to himself, and others, as his Pride, Ambition, Self-Love, Envy, or Revenge, and are subject to the same Humour and Caprice; it is because Nature is *no better* in one Motion than in another, nor can be so, till *something supernatural* is come into it. We often charge Men, both in Church and State, with changing their *Principles*; but the Charge is too hasty; for no Man ever did, or can change his Principles, but by a Birth from above. The *natural*, called in Scripture, the *old Man*, is steadily the same in Heart and Spirit in every Thing he does, whatever Variety of Names may be given to his Actions. For *Self* can have no Motion but what is *selfish*, which Way soever it goes, or whatever it does, either in Church or State. And be assured of this, that *Nature* in every Man, whether he be learned or unlearned, is this *very Self,* and can be nothing else, till a Birth of the Deity is brought forth in it. There is therefore no Possibility of having the Spirit of Love, or any Divine Goodness, from any Power of Nature or Working of Reason. It can only be had in its own Time and Place; and its Time and Place is nowhere, but where Nature is *overcome* by a Birth of the Life of God in the Properties of the Soul. And thus you see the infallible Truth, and absolute

Necessity, of Christian Redemption; it is the most demonstrable Thing in all Nature.— The Deity must become Man, take a Birth in the fallen Nature, be united to it, become the Life of it, or the natural Man must of all Necessity be forever and ever in the Hell of his own Hunger, Anguish, Contrariety, and Self-Torment; and all for this plain Reason, because Nature is, and can be, nothing else, but this Variety of Self-Torment, till the Deity is manifested and dwelling in it.

[Love-1-56] And now, Sir, you see also the absolute Necessity of the Gospel-Doctrine of the Cross, *viz.*, of *dying to Self,* as the one only Way to Life in God. This Cross, or Dying to Self, is the *one Morality* that does Man any Good. Fancy as many Rules as you will of modeling the moral Behaviour of Man, they all do nothing, because they leave Nature still alive, and therefore can only help a Man to a feigned, hypocritical Art of concealing his own inward Evil, and seeming to be not under its Power. And the Reason why it must be so is plain; it is because Nature is not possible to be reformed; it is immutable in its Workings and must be always as it is, and never any better or worse, than its own untaught Workings are. It can no more change from Evil to Good, than Darkness can Work itself into Light. The one Work therefore of Morality is the one Doctrine of the Cross, *viz.*, to resist and deny Nature, that a *supernatural Power* or Divine Goodness, may take Possession of it, and bring a new Light into it.

[Love-1-57] In a Word, there are, in all the Possibility of Things, but two States, or Forms of Life; the one is Nature, and the other is God *manifested in Nature*; and as God and Nature are both within you, so you have it in your Power to live and work with which you will; but are under a Necessity of doing either the one or the other. There is no standing still, Life goes on, and is always bringing forth its *Realities*, which Way soever it goeth. You have seen, that the Properties of Nature are, and can be, nothing else in their own Life, but a *restless Hunger, Disquiet*, and *blind Strife for they know not what*, till the Property of Light and Love has got Possession of them. Now when you see this, you see the *true State* of every natural Man, whether he be *Caesar* or *Cato*, whether he gloriously murders others or only stabs himself; blind Nature does all the Work, and must be the Doer of it, till the *Christ of God* is *born* in him. For the Life of Man can be nothing else but a Hunger of Covetousness, a Rising up of Pride, Envy, and Wrath, a medley of contrary Passions, doing and undoing *it knows not what* because these Workings are *essential* to the Properties of Nature; they must be always hungering, and working one against another, striving to be above one another, and all this in *Blindness*, till the *Light of God* has helped them to *one common Good*, in which they all willingly *unite, rest,* and *rejoice*. In a Word, Goodness is only a *Sound* and Virtue a mere Strife of *natural Passions,* till the *Spirit of Love* is the Breath of every Thing that lives and moves in the Heart. For Love is the one only Blessing and Goodness, and God of Nature; and you have no true Religion, are no Worshiper of the one true God, but in and by that Spirit of Love, which is God himself living and working in you.

[Love-1-58] But here I take off my Pen and shall leave the remaining Part of your Objection to another Opportunity.

King's Cliff, June 16,
1752

Part Two

The First Dialogue Between Theogenes, Eusebius, and Theophilus

[Love-2.1-1] *THEOGENES.* Dear *Theophilus*, this Gentleman is *Eusebius*, a very valuable and worthy Curate in my Neighbourhood; he would not let me wait any longer for your second Letter of the Spirit of Love, nor be content till I consented to our making you this Visit. And indeed, we are both on the same Errand and in equal Impatience to have your full Answer to that Part of my Objection, which you reserved for a second Letter.

[Love-2.1-2] *Theophilus.* My Heart embraces you both with the greatest Affection, and I am much pleased at the Occasion of your Coming which calls me to the most delightful Subject in the World, to help both you and myself to rejoice in that adorable Deity whose infinite Being is an Infinity of mere Love, an unbeginning, never-ceasing, and forever overflowing Ocean of Meekness, Sweetness, Delight, Blessing, Goodness, Patience, and Mercy, and all this as so many blessed Streams breaking out of the Abyss of universal Love, Father, Son, and Holy Ghost, a Triune Infinity of Love and Goodness, for ever and ever giving forth nothing but the same Gifts of Light and Love, of Blessing and Joy, whether before or after the Fall, either of Angels or Men.

[Love-2.1-3] Look at all Nature, through all its Height and Depth, in all its Variety of working Powers; it is what it is for this only End, that the hidden Riches, the invisible Powers, Blessings, Glory, and Love of the unsearchable God, may become visible, sensible, and manifest in and by it.

[Love-2.1-4] Look at all the Variety of Creatures; they are what they are for this only End, that in their infinite Variety, Degrees, and Capacities, they may be as so many speaking Figures, living Forms of the manifold Riches and Powers of Nature, as so many Sounds and Voices, Preachers, and Trumpets, giving Glory and Praise and Thanksgiving to that Deity of Love which gives Life to all Nature and Creature.

[Love-2.1-5] For every Creature of unfallen Nature, call it by what name you Will, has its Form, and Power, and State, and Place in Nature, for no other End, but to open and enjoy, to manifest and rejoice in some Share of the Love, and Happiness, and Goodness of the Deity, as springing forth in the boundless Height and Depth of Nature.

[Love-2.1-6] Now this is the *one Will* and Work of God in and through all Nature and Creature. From Eternity to Eternity he can will and intend nothing toward them, in them, or by them, but the *Communication* of various Degrees of his own Love, Goodness, and Happiness to them, according to their State, and Place, and Capacity in Nature. This is God's unchangeable Disposition toward the Creature; He can be nothing else but all Goodness toward it, because he can be nothing toward the Creature but that which he is, and was, and ever shall be in Himself.

[Love-2.1-7] God can no more begin to have any *Wrath, Rage,* or *Anger* in Himself, after Nature and Creature are in a fallen State, than He could have been infinite Wrath and boundless Rage everywhere, and from all Eternity. For nothing can *begin* to be in God, or to be in a *new State* in Him; every Thing that is in Him is essential to Him, as inseparable from Him, as unalterable in Him as the triune Nature of his Deity.

[Love-2.1-8] *Theogenes*. Pray, *Theophilus*, let me ask you, does not *Patience* and *Pity* and *Mercy* begin to be in God, and only *then begin*, when the Creature has brought itself into Misery? They could have no Existence in the Deity before. Why then may not a Wrath and Anger *begin* to be in God, when the Creature has rebelled against him, though it neither had nor could have any Existence in God before?

[Love-2.1-9] *Theophilus*. 'Tis true, *Theogenes*, that God can only then *begin* to make known his Mercy and Patience, when the Creature has lost its Rectitude and Happiness, yet nothing then begins to be in God or to be found in him, but that which was always in him in the same infinite State, *viz.,* a *Will to all Goodness*, and which *can will nothing else*. And his Patience and Mercy, which could not show forth themselves till Nature and Creature had brought forth Misery, were not new Tempers, or the Beginning of some *new* Disposition that was not in God before, but only *new* and *occasional* Manifestations of that boundless *eternal Will* to *all Goodness*, which always was in God in the same Height and Depth. The Will to all *Goodness*, which is God himself, *began* to display itself in a *new* Way when it first gave Birth to Creatures. The same Will to all Goodness *began* to manifest itself in another *new* Way, when it became Patience and Compassion toward fallen Creatures. But neither of these Ways are the Beginning of any *new Tempers* or Qualities in God, but only new and *occasional Manifestations* of that true eternal Will to all Goodness, which always was, and always will be, in the same Fullness of Infinity in God.

[Love-2.1-10] But to suppose that when the Creature has abused its Power, lost its Happiness and plunged itself into a Misery, out of which it cannot deliver itself, to suppose that then there begins to be *something* in the holy Deity of Father, Son, and Holy Ghost, that is not of the Nature and Essence of God, and which was not there before, *viz.,* a Wrath, and Fury, and vindictive Vengeance, breaking out in Storms of Rage and Resentment because the poor Creature has brought Misery upon itself, is an Impiety and Absurdity that cannot be enough abhorred. For nothing can be in God, but that which He is and has from Himself, and therefore no Wrath can be in the Deity itself, unless God was in Himself, before all Nature, and from all Eternity, an Infinity of Wrath.

[Love-2.1-11] Why are Love, Knowledge, Wisdom, and Goodness said to be infinite and eternal in God, capable of no Increase or Decrease, but always in the same highest State of Existence? Why is his Power eternal and omnipotent, his Presence not here, or there, but everywhere the same? No Reason can be assigned, but because nothing that is *temporary*, *limited*, or bounded, can be in God. It is his Nature to be that which He is, and all that He is, in an infinite, unchangeable Degree, admitting neither higher, nor lower, neither here nor there, but always, and everywhere, in the same unalterable State of Infinity. If therefore Wrath, Rage, and Resentment could be in the Deity itself, it must be an unbeginning, boundless, never-ceasing Wrath, capable of no *more*, or *less*, no *up* or *down*, but always existing, always working, and breaking forth in the same Strength, and everywhere equally burning in the Height and Depth of the abyssal Deity. There is no medium here; there must be either all or none, either no Possibility of Wrath, or no

Possibility of its having any Bounds. And therefore, if you would not say, that every Thing that has proceeded, or can, or ever shall proceed from God, are and can be only so many Effects of his eternal and omnipotent Wrath, which can never cease, or be less than infinite; if you will not hold this monstrous Blasphemy, you must stick close to the absolute Impossibility of Wrath having any Existence in God. For nothing can have any Existence in God, but in the Way and Manner as his Eternity, Infinity, and Omnipotence have their Existence in him. Have you any Thing to object to this?

[Love-2.1-12] *Theogenes.* Indeed, *Theophilus*, both *Eusebius* and myself have been from the first fully satisfied with what has been said of this Matter in the *Book of Regeneration*, the *Appeal*, and the *Spirit of Prayer, &c.* We find it impossible to think of God as subject to Wrath, or capable of being inflamed by the Weakness, and Folly, and Irregularity of the Creature. We find ourselves incapable of thinking any otherwise of God, than as the *one only Good*, or, as you express it, *an eternal immutable Will to all Goodness*, which can will Nothing else to all Eternity, but to communicate Good, and Blessing, and Happiness, and Perfection to every Life, according to its Capacity to receive it.

[Love-2.1-13] Had I an hundred Lives, I could with more Ease part with them, all by suffering an hundred Deaths, than give up this lovely idea of God. Nor could I have any Desire of Eternity for myself, if I had not Hopes, that, by partaking of the Divine Nature, I should be eternally delivered from the Burden and Power of my *own Wrath*, and changed into the blessed *Freedom* of a Spirit, that is *all Love*, and a *mere Will* to Nothing but Goodness. An Eternity without this, is but an Eternity of Trouble. For I know of no Hell, either here or hereafter, but the Power and Working of Wrath, nor any Heaven, but where the God of Love is all in all, and the working Life of all. And therefore, that the holy Deity is all Love, and Blessing, and Goodness, willing and working only Love and Goodness to every Thing, as far as it can receive it, is a Truth as deeply grounded in me as the feeling of my own Existence. I ask you for no Proof of this; my only Difficulty is how to reconcile this Idea of God to the Letter of Scripture. *First*, Because the Scripture speaks so much and so often of the Wrath, and Fury, and vindictive Vengeance of God. *Secondly*, Because the whole Nature of our Redemption is so plainly grounded on such a supposed Degree of Wrath and Vengeance in God, as could not be *satisfied, appeased* and *atoned* by any Thing less than the Death and Sacrifice of the only begotten Son of God.

[Love-2.1-14] *Theophilus.* I will do more for you, *Theogenes*, in this Matter than you seem to expect. I will not only reconcile the Letter of Scripture with the foregoing Description of God, but will show you, that every Thing that is said of the Necessity of Christ's being the only possible *Satisfaction* and *Atonement* of the vindictive Wrath of God is a full and absolute Proof that the Wrath of God spoken of never was, nor is, or possibly can be in God.

[Love-2.1-15] *Eusebius.* Oh! *Theophilus*, you have forced me now to speak, and I cannot contain the Joy that I feel in this Expectation which you have raised in me. If you can make the Scriptures do all that which you have promised to *Theogenes*, I shall be in Paradise before I die. For to know that Love alone was the Beginning of Nature and Creature, that nothing but Love encompasses the whole Universe of Things, that the governing Hand that overrules all, the watchful Eye that sees through all, is nothing but omnipotent and omniscient Love, using an Infinity of Wisdom, to raise all that is fallen in Nature, to save every misguided Creature from the miserable Works of its own Hands, and make Happiness and Glory the perpetual Inheritance of all the Creation is a Reflection that must be quite ravishing to every intelligent Creature that is sensible of it. Thus to think of God, of Providence, and Eternity, whilst we are in this Valley and Shadow of Death, is to have a real Foretaste of the Blessings of the World to come. Pray, therefore, let us hear how the Letter of Scripture is a Proof of this God of Love.

[Love-2.1-16] *Theophilus*. Before I do this, *Eusebius*, I think it requisite to show you, in a Word or two, the true Ground and Nature of Wrath in all its Kinds, what it is in itself, whence it has its Birth, Life, and Manner of Existence. And then you will see with your own Eyes *why*, and *how*, and *where* Wrath or Rage can, or cannot be. And until you see this fundamentally in the Nature of things, you cannot be at all qualified to judge of the Matter in Question, but must only think and speak at random, merely as your Imagination is led by the Sound of Words. For until we know, in the Nature of the Thing, what Wrath is in itself, and *why*, and *how* it comes into Existence, wherever it is, we cannot say, where it can enter or where it cannot. Nor can we possibly know what is meant by the *Satisfaction*, *Appeasement*, or *Atonement* of Wrath in any Being but by knowing *how*, and *why*, and for what Reason Wrath can rise and Work in any Being; and then only can we know how any Wrath, wherever raised, can be *atoned* or made to *cease*.

[Love-2.1-17] Now there are two Things, both of them visible to your outward Senses, which entirely open the *true Ground* and *Nature* of Wrath, and undeniably show what it is in itself, from whence it arises, and wherein its Life, and Strength, and Being consist. And these two Things are, a *Tempest* in the Elements of this World, and a *raging Sore* in the Body of Man, or any other Animal. Now that a Tempest in the Elements is Wrath in the Elements, and a Sore in the Body of an Animal a Wrath in the State of the Juices of the Body, is a Matter, I think, that needs no Proof or Explication. Consider, then, *how* or *why* a Tempest arises in the Elements, or an inflamed Sore in the Body, and then you have the *true Ground* and *Nature* of Wrath. Now a Tempest does not, cannot arise in the Elements whilst they are in their *right State*, in their *just Mixture* or Union with one another. A Sore does not, cannot break forth in the Body, whilst the Body is altogether in its true State and Temperature of its Juices. Hence you plainly see, that Wrath has its *whole Nature*, and *only Ground* of its Existence, in and by the *Disorder* or bad *State* of the Thing in which it exists and works. It can have no Place of Existence, no Power of breaking forth, but where the Thing has *lost* its proper Perfection, and is not as it ought to be. And therefore no good Being, that is in its *proper State* of Goodness, can, whilst it is in such a State, have any Wrath or Rage in it. And therefore, as a Tempest of any kind in the Elements, is a sure Proof that the Elements are not in their right State, but under Disorder, as a *raging Sore* in the Body is a certain Indication that the Body is *impure* and *corrupt*, and not as it should be; so in whatever Mind, or intelligent Being, Wrath or Rage works and breaks forth, there, there is Proof enough, that the Mind is in that same *impure, corrupt,* and *disordered State*, as those Elements that raise a Tempest, and that Body which gives forth an inflamed Sore. And now, Gentlemen, what think you of a supposed Wrath, or Rage in God? Will you have such Things to be in the Deity itself as cannot have Place or Existence even in any Creature, until it is become *disordered* and *impure* and has lost its *proper State* of Goodness?

[Love-2.1-18] *Eusebius*. But pray, *Theophilus*, let me observe, that it does not yet appear to me, that there is but *one* Wrath possible to be in Nature and Creature. I grant there is such a Likeness in the Things you have appealed to, as is sufficient to justify Poets, Orators, or popular Speakers, in calling a Tempest Wrath, and Wrath a Tempest. But this will not do in our present Matter; for all that you have said depends upon this, whether, in a philosophic Strictness in the Nature of the Thing, there can be only *one Wrath*, wherever it is, proceeding strictly from the *same Ground*, and having everywhere the *same Nature*. Now if you can prove this Identity or Sameness of Wrath, be it where it Will, either in an intelligent Mind, the Elements of this World, or the Body of an Animal, then your Point is absolutely gained, and there can be no Possibility for Wrath to have any Existence in the Deity. But as Body and Spirit are generally held to be quite contrary to each other in their most essential Qualities, I do not know how you can sufficiently prove, that they can only have *one Kind* of Wrath, or that Wrath must have *one* and the same Ground and Nature, whether it be in Body or Spirit.

[Love-2.1-19] *Theophilus*. Wrath can have no *better* or other Ground and Nature in Body, than it has in Spirit, for this Reason, because it can have no *Existence* or *Manner* of working in the Body, but what it has *directly* from Spirit. And therefore, in every Wrath that is visible in any *Body* whatever, you have a true Manifestation of the Ground and Nature of Wrath, in whatever Spirit it is. And therefore, as there is but one Ground and Nature of Wrath in all outward Things, whether they be animate or inanimate, so you have Proof enough, that so it is with all Wrath in the Spirit or Mind. Because Wrath in any *Body* or *outward* Thing, is nothing else but the *inward working* of that Spirit, which manifests itself by an outward Wrath in the Body.

[Love-2.1-20] And what we call Wrath in the Body, is truly and strictly speaking, the Wrath of the Spirit in the Body.

[Love-2.1-21] For you are to observe, that *Body* begins not from itself, nor is any Thing of itself, but is all that it is, whether pure or impure, has all that it has, whether of Light or Darkness, and works all that it works, whether of Good or Evil, *merely* from Spirit. For nothing, my Friend, *acts* in the whole Universe of Things but *Spirit alone*. And the State, Condition, and Degree of every Spirit, is only and solely opened by the State, Form, Condition, and Qualities of the Body that belongs to it. For the Body can have no Nature, Form, Condition, or Quality but that which the Spirit that brings it forth, gives to it.

[Love-2.1-22] Was there no *eternal, universal* Spirit, there could be no eternal or universal *Nature*; that is, was not the Spirit of God everywhere, the *Kingdom of Heaven*, or the visible Glory of God, in an outward Majesty of Heaven, could not be everywhere. Now the Kingdom of Heaven is *that* to the Deity, which every *Body* is to the Spirit, which liveth, worketh, and manifesteth itself in it. But the Kingdom of Heaven is not God, yet all that it is, and has, and does, is only an outward Manifestation of the Nature, Power, and Working of the Spirit of God.

[Love-2.1-23] It is thus with every creaturely *Spirit* and its *Body*, which is the Habitation or Seat of its Power; and as the Spirit is in its Nature, Kind and Degree, whether heavenly, earthly, or hellish, so is its Body. Were there not creaturely Spirits, there could be no creaturely Bodies. And the Reason why there are creaturely Bodies of such various Forms, Shapes, and Powers, is because Spirits come forth from God in *various Kinds* and *Degrees* of Life, each manifesting its own Nature, Power, and Condition, by *that Body* which proceeds from it as its *own Birth*, or the Manifestation of its *own Powers*.

[Love-2.1-24] Now the Spirit is not Body, nor is the Body Spirit; they are so *essentially* distinct, that they cannot *possibly* lose their Difference, or be changed into one another; and yet all that is in the Body is from the *Nature, Will*, and *Working* of its Spirit. There is therefore no possible Room for a Supposition of *two Kinds* of Wrath, or that Wrath may have *two Natures*, the one as it is in Spirit, and the other as it is in Body; *first*, because nothing can be wrathful but Spirit, and *secondly*, because no Spirit can exert, or manifest Wrath but in and by its Body. The kindling its *own Body* is the Spirit's *only Wrath*. And therefore, through the whole Universe of Things, there is and can be but *one possible* Ground and Nature of Wrath, whether it be in the *Sore* of an animal Body, in a *Tempest* of the Elements, in the *Mind* of a Man, in an *Angel*, or in *Hell*.

[Love-2.1-25] *Eusebius*. Enough, enough, *Theophilus*. You have made it sufficiently plain, that Wrath can be no more in God Himself than Hell can be Heaven. And therefore we ask no more of you, but only to reconcile this with the Language and Doctrine of the holy Scriptures.

[Love-2.1-26] *Theogenes*. You are in too much Haste, *Eusebius*; it would be better to let *Theophilus* proceed further in this Matter. He has told us what Wrath is in itself, be it where it will; I should be glad to know its *one true* Original, or how, and where, and why it could possibly begin to be.

[Love-2.1-27] *Theophilus*. To inquire or search into the Origin of Wrath, is the same Thing as to search into the Origin of Evil and Sin: For Wrath and Evil are but two Words for one and the same Thing. There is no Evil in any Thing, but the Working of the Spirit of Wrath. And when Wrath is entirely suppressed, there can be no more Evil, or Misery, or Sin in all Nature and Creature. This therefore is a firm Truth, that nothing can be capable of Wrath, or be the Beginning of Wrath, but the Creature, because nothing but the Creature can be the Beginner of Evil and Sin.

[Love-2.1-28] Again, the Creature can have *no Beginning*, or Sensibility of Wrath in itself, but by *losing* the living Power, the living Presence, and governing Operation of the Spirit of God within it; or in other Words, by its losing that heavenly State of Existence in God, and Influence from Him which it had at its Creation.

[Love-2.1-29] Now no intelligent Creature, whether Angel or Man, can be *good* and *happy* but by partaking of, or having in itself, a *two-fold* Life. Hence so much is said in the Scripture of an inward and outward, an old and a new Man.— For there could be no Foundation for this Distinction, but because every intelligent Creature, created to be good and happy, must of all *Necessity* have a two-fold Life in it, or it cannot possibly be capable of Goodness and Happiness, nor can it possibly lose its Goodness and Happiness, or feel the least Want of them, but by its breaking the *Union* of this two-fold Life in itself. Hence so much is said in the Scripture of the quickening, raising, and reviving the inward, new Man, of the new Birth from above, of Christ being formed in us, as the one only Redemption and Salvation of the Soul. Hence also the Fall of *Adam* was said to be a *Death*, that he died the Day of his Sin, though he lived so many hundred Years after it: it was because his Sin broke the *Union* of his two-fold Life and put an End to the heavenly Part of it, and left only *one Life*, the Life of this bestial, earthly World in him.

[Love-2.1-30] Now there is, in the Nature of the Thing, an absolute Necessity of this *two-fold Life* in every Creature that is to be *good* and *happy*; and the two-fold Life is this, it must have the Life of *Nature*, and the Life of *God* in it. It cannot be a Creature, and intelligent, but by having the Life and Properties of *Nature*; that is, by finding itself to be a Life of *various Sensibilities*, that hath a Power of *Understanding, Willing*, and *Desiring*: This is its *creaturely* Life, which, by the creating Power of God, it hath in and from Nature.

[Love-2.1-31] Now this is all the Life that is, or can be *creaturely*, or be a Creature's *natural, own* Life; and all this creaturely natural Life, with all its various Powers and Sensibilities, is only a Life of *various Appetites, Hungers*, and *Wants*, and cannot possibly be any Thing else. God Himself cannot make a Creature to be in *itself*, or as to its *own Nature*, any Thing else but a State of *Emptiness*, of *Want*, of *Appetite, &c.* He cannot make it to be good and happy, *in* and *from* its natural State: This is as impossible as for God to cease to be the *one only Good*. The highest Life, therefore, that is natural and creaturely, can go no higher than this; it can only be a *bare Capacity* for Goodness and Happiness, and cannot possibly be a good and happy Life, but by the Life of God dwelling in, and in Union with it. And this is the two-fold Life, that of *all Necessity* must be *united* in every good and perfect and happy Creature.

[Love-2.1-32] See here the greatest of all Demonstrations of the absolute Necessity of the Gospel Redemption and Salvation, and all proved from the Nature of the Thing. There can be no Goodness and Happiness for any intelligent Creature, but in and by this two-fold Life; and therefore the *Union* of the Divine and human Life, or the Son of God incarnate in Man, to make Man again a Partaker of the Divine Nature, is the *one only* possible Salvation for all the Sons of fallen *Adam*, that is, of *Adam* dead to, or fallen from his first Union with the Divine Life.

[Love-2.1-33] *Deism*, therefore, or a Religion of Nature, pretending to make Man good and happy without Christ, or the Son of God entering into *Union* with the human Nature, is the greatest of all Absurdities. It is as contrary to the Nature and Possibilities of Things as for mere *Emptiness* to be its own Fullness, mere *Hunger* to be its own Food, and mere *Want* to be its Possession of all Things. For Nature and Creature, without the Christ of God or the Divine Life in Union with it, is and can be nothing else but this mere *Emptiness, Hunger*, and *Want* of all that which can alone make it good and happy. For God himself, as I said, cannot make any Creature to be good and happy by any Thing that is in its own created Nature; and however high and noble any Creature is supposed to be created, its Height and Nobility can consist in nothing, but its higher Capacity and Fitness to receive a higher Union with the Divine Life, and also a higher and more wretched Misery, when left to itself, as is manifest by the hellish State of the fallen Angels. Their high and exalted Nature was only an enlarged Capacity for the Divine Life; and therefore, when this Life was lost, their whole created Nature was nothing else but the Height of Rage, and hellish Distraction.

[Love-2.1-34] A plain Demonstration, that there can be no Happiness, Blessing, and Goodness for any Creature in Heaven, or on Earth, but by having, as the Gospel saith, Jesus Christ made unto it, *Wisdom, Righteousness*, Sanctification, and Peace with God.

[Love-2.1-35] And the Reason is this; it is because Goodness and Happiness are absolutely inseparable from God, and can be nowhere but in God. And on the other Hand, *Emptiness, Want,*

Insufficiency, &c., are absolutely inseparable from the Creature, as such; its whole Nature cannot possibly be any Thing else, be it what or where it will, an Angel in Heaven, or a Man on Earth; it is and must be, in its *whole creaturely* Nature and Capacity, a mere Hunger and Emptiness, *&c.* And therefore all that we know of God, and all that we know of the Creature, fully proves, that the *Life of God* in Union with the *creaturely Life* (which is the Gospel Salvation) is the one only Possibility of Goodness and Happiness in any Creature, whether in Heaven or on Earth.

[Love-2.1-36] Hence also it is enough certain, that this *two-fold Life* must have been the *original State* of every intelligent Creature, at its first coming forth from God. It could not be brought forth by God, to have only a *creaturely Life* of Nature, and be left to that; for that would be creating it under a *Necessity* of being in Misery, in Want, in Wrath, and all painful Sensibilities. A Thing more unworthy of God, and more impossible for Him to do, than to create numberless earthly Animals under a Necessity of being perpetually pained with Hunger and Thirst, without any Possibility of finding any Thing to eat or to drink.

[Love-2.1-37] For no creaturely Life can in itself be any higher, or better, than a State of Want, or a seeking for something that cannot be found in itself; and therefore, as sure as God is good, as sure as He would have intelligent Beings live a Life of Goodness and Happiness, so sure it is, that such Beings must of all Necessity, in their first Existence, have been blessed with a *two-fold Life, viz.,* the Life of God dwelling in, and united with, the Life of Nature or created Life.

[Love-2.1-38] *Eusebius.* What an important Matter have you here proved, in the Necessity and Certainty of this *two-fold* Life in every intelligent Being that is to be good and happy: For this great Truth opens and asserts the certain and substantial Ground of the spiritual Life, and shows, that all Salvation is, and can be nothing else, but the *Manifestation* of the Life of God in the Soul. How clearly does this give the solid Distinction between inward Holiness, and all outward, creaturely Practices. All that God has done for Man by any particular Dispensations, whether by the *Law,* or the *Prophets,* by the *Scriptures,* or *Ordinances* of the Church, are only as Helps to a Holiness which they cannot give, but are only suited to the Death and Darkness of the earthly, creaturely Life, to turn it from itself, from its own Workings, and awaken in it a Faith and Hope, a Hunger and Thirst after that *first Union* with the Life of the Deity, which was lost in the Fall of the first Father of Mankind.

[Love-2.1-39] How unreasonable is it, to call *perpetual Inspiration* Fanaticism and Enthusiasm, when there cannot be the *least Degree* of Goodness or Happiness in any intelligent Being, but what is in its whole Nature, merely and truly the *Breathing,* the *Life,* and the *Operation* of God in the Life of the Creature? For if Goodness can only be in God, if it cannot exist *separate* from Him, if He can only *bless* and *sanctify,* not by a creaturely gift, but by *Himself* becoming the *Blessing* and *Sanctification* of the Creature, then it is the highest Degree of Blindness, to look for any Goodness and Happiness from any Thing, but the *immediate Indwelling Union,* and *Operation* of the Deity in the Life of the Creature. Perpetual Inspiration, therefore, is in the Nature of the Thing as necessary to a Life of Goodness, Holiness, and Happiness, as the perpetual Respiration of the Air is necessary to Animal Life.

[Love-2.1-40] For the Life of the Creature, whilst only creaturely, and possessing nothing but itself, is Hell; that is, it is all *Pain* and Want and *Distress.* Now nothing, in the Nature of the

Thing, can make the *least Alteration* in this creaturely Life, nothing can help it to be in *Light* and *Love*, in *Peace* and *Goodness*, but the Union of God with it, and the Life of God working in it, because nothing but God is Light, and Love, and heavenly Goodness. And, therefore, where the Life of God is not become the Life and Goodness of the Creature, there the Creature cannot have the least Degree of Goodness in it.

[Love-2.1-41] What a mistake is it, therefore, to confine Inspiration to *particular* Times and Occasions, to Prophets and Apostles, and extraordinary Messengers of God, and to call it *Enthusiasm,* when the common Christian looks, and trusts to be *continually led* and inspired by the Spirit of God! For though all are not called to be Prophets or Apostles, yet all are called to be *holy,* as He who has called them is *holy, to be perfect as their heavenly Father is perfect, to be like-minded with Christ,* to will only as God wills, to do all to his Honour and Glory, to renounce the Spirit of this World, to have their Conversation in Heaven, to set their Affections on Things above, to love God with all their Heart, Soul, and Spirit, and their Neighbour as themselves.

[Love-2.1-42] Behold a Work as *great,* as *Divine* and *supernatural,* as that of a Prophet and an Apostle. But to suppose that we ought, and may always be in this Spirit of Holiness, and yet are not, and ought not to be *always moved and led by the Breath and Spirit of God within us,* is to suppose that there is a Holiness and Goodness which comes not from God; which is no better than supposing that there may be true Prophets and Apostles who have not their Truth from God.

[Love-2.1-43] Now the Holiness of the common Christian is not an *occasional* Thing, that begins and ends, or is only for such a Time, or Place, or Action, but is the Holiness of *that,* which is always *alive* and *stirring* in us, namely, of our Thoughts, Wills, Desires, and Affections. If therefore these are always alive in us, always driving or governing our Lives, if we can have no Holiness or Goodness, but as this Life of Thought, Will, and Affection works in us, if we are all called to this inward Holiness and Goodness, then a *perpetual, always-existing Operation of the Spirit of God within us,* is absolutely necessary. For we cannot be inwardly led and governed by a Spirit of Goodness, but by being governed by the *Spirit of God himself.* For the Spirit of God and the Spirit of Goodness are not two Spirits, nor can we be said to have any more of the one, than we have of the other.

[Love-2.1-44] Now if our Thoughts, Wills, and Affections, need only be now and then holy and good, then, indeed, the moving and breathing Spirit of God need only now and then govern us. But if our Thoughts and Affections are to be always holy and good, then the holy and good Spirit of God is to be always operating, as a Principle of Life within us.

[Love-2.1-45] The Scripture saith, "We are not sufficient of ourselves to think a good Thought." If so, then we cannot be chargeable with not thinking, and willing that which is good, but upon this *Supposition*, that there is always a *supernatural* Power within us, ready and able to help us to the Good which we cannot have from ourselves.

[Love-2.1-46] The Difference then of a good and a bad Man does not lie in this, that the one wills that which is good, and the other does not, but solely in this, that the one concurs with the living inspiring Spirit of God within him and the other resists it, and is and can be *only chargeable* with Evil, because he resists it.

[Love-2.1-47] Therefore whether you consider that which is good or bad in a Man, they equally prove the *perpetual Indwelling* and *Operation* of the Spirit of God within us, since we can only be bad by resisting, as we are good by yielding to the Spirit of God; both which equally suppose a perpetual Operation of the Spirit of God within us.

[Love-2.1-48] How firmly our established Church adheres to this Doctrine of the Necessity of the *perpetual Operation* of the Holy Spirit, as the one only Source and Possibility of any Degree of Divine Light, Wisdom, Virtue, and Goodness in the Soul of Man, how earnestly she wills and requires all her Members to live in the most open Profession of it, and in the highest Conformity to it, may be seen by many such Prayers as these, in her common, ordinary, public Service.

[Love-2.1-49] "O God, forasmuch as without Thee we are not able to please Thee, grant that thy Holy Spirit may in all Things direct and rule our Hearts." Again, "We pray Thee, that thy Grace may ALWAYS prevent and follow us, and make us CONTINUALLY to be given to all good Works." Again, "Grant to us, Lord, we beseech Thee, the Spirit to think and do ALWAYS such things as be rightful, that we, who cannot do anything that is good without Thee, may by Thee be enabled to live according to thy Will." Again, "Because the Frailty of Man, without Thee cannot but Fall, keep us ever, by thy Help from all Things hurtful, and lead us to all Things profitable to our Salvation," &c. Again, "O God, from whom all good Things do come, grant to us thy humble Servants, that by thy holy inspiration we may think those Things that be good, and by thy merciful guiding may perform the same."— But now the *true Ground* of all this Doctrine of the Necessity of the perpetual Guidance and Operation of the Holy Spirit, lies in what has been said above, of the Necessity of a *two-fold Life* in every intelligent Creature that is to be good and happy. For if the creaturely Life, whilst alone, or left to itself, can only be *Want, Misery,* and *Distress,* if it cannot possibly have any Goodness or Happiness in it, till the Life of God is *in Union* with it, *as one Life,* then every Thing that you read in the Scripture of the Spirit of God, as the only Principle of Goodness, opens itself to you as a most certain and blessed Truth, about which you can have no doubt.

[Love-2.1-50] *Theophilus.* Let me only add, *Eusebius,* to what you have said, that from this absolute Necessity of a *two-fold Life,* in every Creature, that is, to be good and happy, we may, in a still greater Clearness see the Certainty of that which we have so often spoken of at other Times, namely, that the *inspoken Word* in Paradise, the *Bruiser* of the Serpent, the *Seed* of the Woman, the *Immanuel,* the holy Jesus (for they all mean the same Thing) is, and was the only possible Ground of Salvation for fallen Man. For if the two-fold Life is necessary, and Man could not be restored to Goodness and Happiness but by the *restored Union* of this two-fold Life into its first State, then there was an absolute Necessity in the Nature of the Thing, that every Son of Adam should have such a *Seed of Heaven* in the Birth of his Life, as could, by the *Mediation* of Christ, be raised into a Birth and Growth of the first perfect Man. This is the one Original Power of Salvation, without which, no external Dispensation could have done any Thing towards raising the fallen State of Man. For nothing could be raised, but what *there* was to be raised, nor Life be given to any Thing but to that which was capable of Life. Unless, therefore, there had been a *Seed of Life,* or a smothered Spark of Heaven in the Soul of Man, which wanted to come to the Birth, there had been no Possibility for any Dispensation of God, to bring forth a Birth of Heaven in fallen Man.

[Love-2.1-51] The *Faith* of the first *Patriarchs* could not have been in Being; *Moses* and the *Prophets* had come in vain, had not the Christ of God lain in a *State of Hiddenness* in every Son of Man. For *Faith*, which is a Will and Hunger after God, could not have *begun* to be, or have any Life in Man, but because there was something of the Divine Nature *existing* and *hid* in Man. For nothing can have any longing Desire but after its own Likeness, nor could any Thing be made to Desire God, but that which came from Him, and had the Nature of Him.

[Love-2.1-52] The whole mediatorial Office of Christ, from his Birth to his sitting down in Power at the right Hand of God, was only for this End, to help Man to a Life that was fallen into *Death* and Insensibility in him. And therefore his mediatorial Power was to manifest itself by Way of a *new Birth*. In the Nature of the Thing nothing else was to be done, and Christ had no other Way to proceed, and that for this plain Reason, because Life was the Thing that was lost, and Life, wherever it is, must be raised by a Birth, and every Birth must, and can only come from its *own Seed*.

[Love-2.1-53] But if Christ was to raise a new Life like his own in every Man, then every Man must have had originally, in the inmost Spirit of his Life, a *Seed* of Christ, or Christ as a Seed of Heaven, lying there as in a State of *Insensibility* or *Death*, out of which it could not arise but by the *mediatorial Power* of Christ, who, as a second Adam, was to regenerate that Birth of his *own Life*, which was *lost* in all the natural Sons of Adam the first.

[Love-2.1-54] But unless there was this *Seed* of *Christ,* or Spark of Heaven hidden in the Soul, not the least Beginning of Man's Salvation, or of Christ's mediatorial Office could be made. For *what* could begin to deny *Self,* if there was not something in Man *different* from Self? What could begin to have *Hope* and *Faith* and Desire of an heavenly Life, if there was not *something* of *Heaven hidden* in his Soul, and lying therein, as in a State of Inactivity and Death, till raised by the Mediation of Christ into its first Perfection of Life, and set again in its true Dominion over Flesh and Blood?

[Love-2.1-55] *Eusebius*. You have, *Theophilus*, sufficiently proved the Certainty and Necessity of this Matter. But I should be glad if you knew how to help me to some more distinct Idea and Conception of it.

[Love-2.1-56] *Theophilus*. An Idea is not the Thing to be here sought for; it would rather hinder, than help your true Knowledge of it. But perhaps the following Similitude may be of some Use to you.

[Love-2.1-57] The *Ten Commandments,* when written by God on Tables of Stone, and given to Man, did not then first begin to belong to Man; they had their *Existence* in Man, were *born* with him, they lay as a *Seed* and *Power* of Goodness, *hidden* in the Form and Make of his Soul, and altogether inseparable from it, before they were shown to Man on *Tables of Stone*. And when they were shown to Man on Tables of Stone, they were only an *outward Imitation* of that which was inwardly in Man, though not *legible* because of that Impurity of Flesh and Blood, in which they were drowned and swallowed up. For the earthly Nature, having overcome the Divinity that was in Man, it gave Commandments of *its own* to Man, and required Obedience to all the Lusts of the Flesh, the Lust of the Eyes, and the Pride of Life.

[Love-2.1-58] Hence it became necessary, that God should give an *outward* Knowledge of such Commandments as were become inwardly *unknown, unfelt,* and, as it were, shut up in Death in the Soul.

[Love-2.1-59] But now, had not *all* that is in these Commandments been *really* and *antecedently* in the Soul, as its *own Birth* and *Nature,* had they not still *lain therein,* and, although totally suppressed, yet in such a *Seed* or *Remains,* as could be called forth into their first living State, in vain had the Tables of Stone been given to Man; and all outward Writing, or Teaching of the Commandments, had been as useless, as so many Instructions given to *Beasts* or *Stones.* If therefore you can conceive, how all that is *good* and *holy* in the Commandments, lay *hid* as an *unfelt, unactive* Power or *Seed* of Goodness, till called into Sensibility and stirring by Laws written on Tables of Stone, this may help your Manner of conceiving, and believing, how Christ as a *Seed* of Life or *Power* of Salvation, lies in the Soul as *its unknown, hidden Treasure,* till awakened and called forth into Life by the *mediatorial* Office and Process of the holy Jesus.

[Love-2.1-60] Again, "Thou shalt love the Lord thy God with all thy Heart, with all thy Soul, and with all thy Strength, and thy Neighbour as thyself." Now these two Precepts, given by the written Word of God, are an absolute Demonstration of the *first original* Perfection of Man, and also a full and invincible Proof, that the same original Perfection is not quite *annihilated,* but lies in him as a *hidden, suppressed Seed* of Goodness, capable of being raised up to its first Perfection. For had not this Divine *Unity, Purity,* and *Perfection* of Love toward God and Man, been Man's *first natural* State of Life, it could have nothing to do with his present State. For had any other Nature, or Measure, or kind of Love begun in the first Birth of his Life, he could only have been called to that. For no Creature has, or can have a Call to be above, or act above its own Nature. Therefore, as sure as Man is called to this Unity, Purity, and Perfection of Love, so sure is it, that it was, at first, his natural, heavenly State, and still has its *Seed,* or *Remains* within him, as his only Power and Possibility of rising up to it again. And therefore, all that Man is called to, every Degree of a new and perfect Life, every future Exaltation and Glory he is to have from the Mediation of Christ, is a full Proof, that the same Perfection was originally his natural State, and is *still* in him in *such a Seed* or *Remains* of Existence, as to admit of a perfect Renewal.

[Love-2.1-61] And thus it is, that you are to conceive of the holy Jesus, or the Word of God, as the *hidden Treasure* of every human Soul, born as a *Seed* of the Word in the Birth of the Soul, immured under Flesh and Blood, *till as a Day-Star, it arises in our Hearts,* and changes the Son of an earthly Adam into a Son of God.

[Love-2.1-62] And was not the Word and Spirit of God in us all, antecedent to any *Dispensation* or *written* Word of God, as a *real* Seed of Life in the Birth of our own Life, we could have no more Fitness for the Gospel-Redemption, than the Animals of this World, which have nothing of Heaven in them. And to call us to Love God with all our Hearts, to *put on Christ,* to walk *according to* the Spirit, if these Things had not their *real Nature* and *Root* within us, would be as vain and useless, as to make Rules and Orders how our Eyes should smell and taste, or our Ears should see.

[Love-2.1-63] Now this Mystery of an *inward Life hidden* in Man, as his most precious Treasure, as the Ground of all that can be great or good in him, and hidden only since his Fall, and which only can be opened and brought forth in its first Glory by Him to whom all Power in Heaven and on Earth is given, is a Truth to which almost every Thing in Nature bears full Witness. Look where you will, nothing appears, or works *outwardly* in any Creature, or in any Effect of Nature, but what is all done from its *own inward invisible Spirit,* not a Spirit brought into it, but its *own inward* Spirit, which is an inward invisible Mystery, till made known, or brought forth by outward Appearances.

[Love-2.1-64] The Sea neither is, nor can be moved and tossed by any other Wind, than that which hath its Birth, and Life, and Strength, in and from the Sea itself, as its *own Wind*. The Sun in the Firmament gives Growth to every Thing that grows in the Earth, and Life to every Thing that lives upon it, not by giving or imparting a Life *from without*, but only by stirring up in every Thing its *own Growth,* and its *own Life,* which lay as in a *Seed* or *State* of Death, till helped to come out of it by the Sun, which, as an Emblem of the Redeemer of the spiritual World, helps every earthly Thing out of its own Death into its *own highest* State of Life.

[Love-2.1-65] That which we call our Sensations, as *seeing, hearing, feeling, tasting*, and *smelling*, are not Things brought into us from without, or given unto us by any external Causes, but are only so many *inborn, secret States* of the Soul, which lie in their *State of Hiddenness* till they are occasionally awakened, and brought forth into Sensibility by outward Occurrences. And were they not *antecedently* in the Soul, as *States* and *Forms* of its own Life, no outward Objects could bring the Soul into a Sensibility of them. For nothing can have, or be in any State of Sensation, but that which it is, and hath from itself, as its own Birth. This is as certain as that a Circle hath only its *own Roundness*.

[Love-2.1-66] The *stinking Gum* gives nothing to the Soul, nor brings any Thing into Sensibility but that which was before in the Soul; it has only a Fitness to awaken, and stir up *that State* of the Soul, which *lay dormant before*, and which when brought into Sensibility, is called the Sensation of bad Smelling. And the *odoriferous Gum* hath likewise but the same Power, *viz.,* a Fitness to stir up *that State* of Sensation in the Soul, which is called its delightful Smelling. But both these Sensations are only *internal States* of the Soul, which *appear*, or disappear, are *found*, or not found, just as Occasions bring them into Sensibility.

[Love-2.1-67] Again, the greatest Artist in *Music* can add *no Sound* to his Instrument, nor make it give forth any other Melody, but that which lieth *silently hidden in it,* as its own inward State.

[Love-2.1-68] Look now at what you will, whether it be animate, or inanimate: All that it is, or has, or can be, it is and has in and from itself, as its *own inward State*; and all outward Things can do no more to it, than the Hand does to the Instrument, make it show forth its *own inward* State, either of Harmony or Discord.

[Love-2.1-69] It is strictly thus with ourselves. Not a Spark of *Joy*, of *Wrath*, of *Envy*, of *Love* or *Grief,* can possibly enter into us from *without*, or be caused to be *in us* by any *outward* Thing. This is as impossible, as for the Sound of *Metals* to be put into a *Lump* of Clay. And as no *Metal* can possibly give forth any other, or higher Sound, than that which is enclosed within it, so we, however struck, can give forth no other or higher Sound either of *Love, Hatred, Wrath, &c.*, than that *very Degree* which lay before shut up within us.

[Love-2.1-70] The *natural State* of our Tempers has Variety of Covers, under which they lie concealed at Times, both from ourselves and others; but when this or that Accident happens to *displace* such or such a Cover, then that which lay hid under it breaks forth. And then we vainly think, that this or that outward Occasion has not shown us how we are within, but has only *infused* or *put* into us a Wrath, or Grief, or Envy, which is not *our natural State* or of our *own Growth*, or has all that it has from our own inward State.

[Love-2.1-71] But this is mere Blindness and Self-Deceit, for it is as impossible for the Mind to have any Grief, or Wrath, or Joy, but what it has all from its *own inward State*, as for the Instrument to give forth any other Harmony, or Discord, but that which is within and from itself.

[Love-2.1-72] Persons, Things, and outward Occurrences may strike our Instrument improperly, and variously, but as we are in ourselves, such is our outward Sound, whatever strikes us.

[Love-2.1-73] If our inward State is the *renewed Life* of Christ within us, then every Thing and Occasion, let it be what it will, only makes the *same Life* to sound forth, and show itself; then if one Cheek is smitten, we meekly turn the other also. But if Nature is alive and only under a *religious Cover*, then every outward Accident that shakes or disturbs this Cover, gives Leave to that *bad State*, whether of Grief, or Wrath, or Joy that *lay hid* within us, to show forth itself.

[Love-2.1-74] But nothing at any Time makes the least Show, or Sound outwardly, but only that which lay ready within us, for an outward Birth, as Occasion should offer.

[Love-2.1-75] What a miserable Mistake is it therefore, to place religious Goodness in outward Observances, in Notions, and Opinions, which good and bad Men can equally receive and practise, and to treat the *ready real Power and Operation of an inward Life of God in the Birth of our Souls* as Fanaticism and Enthusiasm, when not only the whole Letter and Spirit of Scripture, but every Operation in Nature and Creature demonstrates that the Kingdom of Heaven must be *all within* us, or it never can possibly belong to us. Goodness, Piety, and Holiness, can only be ours, as thinking, willing, and desiring are ours, by being in us, as a Power of Heaven in the Birth and Growth of our own Life.

[Love-2.1-76] And now, *Eusebius*, how is the great controversy about Religion and Salvation shortened.

[Love-2.1-77] For since the *one only* Work of Christ as your Redeemer is only this, to take from the earthly Life of Flesh and Blood its usurped Power, and to raise the smothered Spark of Heaven out of its State of Death, into a powerful governing Life of the whole Man, your *one only* Work also under your Redeemer is fully known. And you have the utmost Certainty, *what* you are to do, *where* you are to seek, and in *what* you are to *find* your Salvation. All that you have to *do*, or can do, is to oppose, resist, and, as far as you can, to renounce the evil Tempers, and Workings of your own earthly Nature. You are under the Power of no other Enemy, are held in no other Captivity, and want no other Deliverance, but from the Power of your *own earthly Self*. This is the one Murderer of the Divine Life within you. It is your own *Cain* that murders your own *Abel*. Now every Thing that your earthly Nature does, is under the Influence of *Self-will*, *Self-love*, and *Self-seeking*, whether it carries you to laudable or blamable Practices, all is done in the Nature and Spirit of *Cain* and only helps you to such Goodness, as when *Cain* slew his Brother. For every Action and Motion of *Self* has the Spirit of *Anti-christ* and murders the Divine Life within you.

[Love-2.1-78] Judge not therefore of your Self, by considering how many of those Things you do, which *Divines* and *Moralists* call Virtue and Goodness, nor how much you abstain from those Things, which they call Sin and Vice.

[Love-2.1-79] But daily and hourly, in every Step that you take, see to the *Spirit that is within you,* whether it be Heaven, or Earth that guides you. And judge every Thing to be Sin and Satan, in which your *earthly Nature, own Love,* or *Self-seeking* has any Share of Life in you; nor think that any Goodness is brought to Life in you, but so far as it is an *actual Death* to the Pride, the Vanity, the Wrath, and selfish Tempers of your fallen, earthly Life.

[Love-2.1-80] Again, here you see, *where* and how you are to seek your Salvation, not in taking up your traveling Staff, or crossing the Seas to find out a new *Luther* or a new *Calvin,* to clothe yourself with their Opinions. No. The *Oracle* is at Home, that *always* and *only* speaks the Truth to you, because nothing is *your Truth,* but that Good and that Evil which is yours within you. For Salvation or Damnation is no outward Thing, that is brought into you from without, but is only *That* which springs up within you, as the Birth and State of your own Life. What you are in yourself, what is doing in yourself, is all that can be either your Salvation or Damnation.

[Love-2.1-81] For all that is our Good and all that is our Evil, has no Place nor Power but within us. Again, nothing that we do is bad, but for this Reason, because it *resists* the Power and working of God *within* us; and nothing that we do can be good but because it conforms to the Spirit of God *within* us. And therefore, as all that can be Good, and all that can be Evil in us, necessarily supposes a God *working within us,* you have the utmost Certainty that God, Salvation, and the Kingdom of Heaven, are nowhere to be sought, or found, but within you, and that all *outward Religion* from the Fall of Man to this Day, is not for itself, but merely for the Sake of an *inward* and *Divine* Life, which was lost when *Adam* died his first Death in Paradise. And therefore it may well be said, that *Circumcision is nothing,* and *Uncircumcision is nothing,* because nothing is wanted, and therefore nothing can be available, but the *new Creature* called out of its Captivity under the Death and Darkness of Flesh and Blood, into the Light, Life, and Perfection of its first Creation.

[Love-2.1-82] And thus also, you have the fullest Proof in *what* your Salvation precisely consists. Not in any historic Faith, or Knowledge of any Thing absent or distant from you, not in any Variety of Restraints, Rules, and Methods of practising Virtues, not in any *Formality* of Opinion about *Faith* and *Works, Repentance, Forgiveness* of *Sins,* or *Justification* and *Sanctification,* not in any Truth or Righteousness, that you can have from yourself, from the best of Men or Books, but wholly and solely in the *Life of God,* or Christ of God *quickened* and born again in you, or in other Words, in the Restoration and perfect Union of the first *two-fold Life* in the Humanity.

[Love-2.1-83] *Theogenes.* Though all that has passed betwixt you and *Eusebius,* concerns Matters of the greatest Moment, yet I must call it a Digression, and quite useless to me. For I have not the least Doubt about any of these Things you have been asserting. It is visible enough, that there can be no *Medium* in this Matter; either Religion must be all *spiritual* or all *carnal*; that is, we must either take up with the Grossness of the *Sadducees,* who say there is neither Angel nor Spirit, or with such Purification as the *Pharisees* had from their washing of Pots and Vessels, and tithing their Mint and Rue; we must, I say, either acquiesce in all this Carnality, or we must profess a Religion that is *all Spirit and Life*, and merely for the sake of raising up an *inward spiritual Life* of Heaven that fell into Death in our first Father.

[Love-2.1-84] I consent also to every Thing that you have said of the Nature and Origin of Wrath. That it can have no Place, nor Possibility of Beginning, but solely in the *creaturely Nature*, nor even any Possibility of Beginning there, till the Creature has died to, or lost its *proper State* of Existence in God; that is, till it has lost that Life, and Blessing, and Happiness, which it had in and from God at its first Creation.

[Love-2.1-85] But I still ask, what must I do with all those Scriptures, which not only make God capable of being provoked to Wrath and Resentment, but frequently inflamed with the highest Degrees of Rage, Fury, and Vengeance, that can be expressed by Words?

[Love-2.1-86] *Theophilus*. I promised, you know, to remove this Difficulty, and will be as good as my Word. But I must first tell you, that you are in much more Distress about it than you need to be. For in the little Book of *Regeneration*, in the *Appeal*, in the *Spirit of Prayer, &c.*, which you have read with such entire Approbation, the whole Matter is cleared up from its true Ground, how *Wrath* in the Scriptures is ascribed to God, and yet cannot belong to the Nature of the Deity.

[Love-2.1-87] Thus you are told in the Appeal, *After these two Falls of two orders of Creatures* (that is, of Angels and Man), *the Deity itself* came to have new and strange *Names*, new and unheard of *Tempers* and *Inclinations* of Wrath, Fury, and Vengeance *ascribed to it*. *I call them new, because they began at the Fall;* I call them strange *because they were foreign to the Deity, and could not belong to God in Himself. Thus, God is said to be a* consuming Fire. But to whom? *To the fallen Angels and lost Souls. But* why, and how, *is He* so to them? *It is because those Creatures have lost all that they had from God but* the Fire of their Nature, and *therefore God can only be* found and manifested *in them* as a consuming Fire. *Now, is it not justly said, that God, who is nothing but infinite Love, is yet in such Creatures* only a consuming Fire? *And though God be nothing but Love, yet they are under the Wrath* and Vengeance of God *because they have only* that Fire *in them which is broken off from the Light and Love of God and so can* know or feel *nothing of God but his* Fire of Nature *in* them. *As Creatures, they can have no Life but what they have* in and from God; and *therefore that wrathful* Life which they have, is truly said to be *a* Wrath or Fire of God *upon* them. *And yet it is still strictly true that there is no Wrath* in God Himself, *that He is not changed in his Temper toward the Creatures, that he does not cease to be one and the same* infinite Fountain *of Goodness*, infinitely flowing forth *in the Riches of his Love* upon all and every Life. (Now, Sir, mind what follows, as the true Ground, how Wrath can and cannot be ascribed to God.) God is not changed from Love to Wrath, *but the Creatures have changed* their *own State* in Nature, *and so the God of Nature can only be manifested in them*, according to *their own State in Nature*. And, *N.B.*, this is the true Ground of *rightly understanding all that is said* of the Wrath and Vengeance *of God in and upon the Creatures. It is only* in such a Sense, as the Curse of God *may be said to be upon them, not because any Thing* cursed *can* be in *or come* from God, *but because they have made* that Life, *which they must have* in God, *to be* a mere Curse to *themselves.* For *every Creature that lives must have its Life* in and from *God, and therefore God must be in every Creature. This is* as *true* of Devils, as of holy Angels. But how is God in them? *N.B.* Why, only as *He is manifested in Nature.* Holy Angels have the Triune Life of God, as manifested in *Nature,* so *manifested also in them,* and *therefore God is in them all* Love, Goodness, Majesty, and Glory, and *theirs* is the *Kingdom of Heaven.*

[Love-2.1-88] *Devils have* nothing *of this Triune Life left in them,* but the Fire, or *Wrath of eternal Nature,* broken off *from all* Light and Love; *and therefore the Life that they can have in and from God* is only and solely *a Life* of Wrath, Rage, and Darkness, and *theirs* is *the Kingdom of Hell.*

[Love-2.1-89] *And because this Life,* (though all Rage and Darkness*), is a Strength and Power of Life, which they must have in and from God,* and *which they cannot take out of his Hands,* therefore *is their* cursed, miserable, wrathful Life, *truly* and *justly said to be* the Curse and Misery, and Wrath, and Vengeance of God *upon them, though God Himself* can no *more have Curse, Misery, Wrath, and Vengeance* than He can have Mischief, Malice, or any fearful Tremblings in his holy Triune Deity.

[Love-2.1-90] See now, *Theogenes,* what little Occasion you had for your present Difficulty. For here, in the above cited Words, which you have been several Years acquainted with, the true Ground and Reason is plainly shown you, *how* and *why* all the *Wrath, Rage,* and *Curse* that is anywhere stirring in Nature, or breaking forth in any Creature, is and must be in all Truth called by the Scriptures the Wrath, and Rage, and Vengeance of God, though it be the greatest of all Impossibilities for Rage and Wrath to be in the Holy Deity itself.

[Love-2.1-91] The Scriptures therefore are literally true in all that they affirm of the Wrath, *&c.,* of God. For is it not as literally true of God, that Hell and Devils are his, as that Heaven and holy Angels are his? Must not therefore all the Wrath and Rage of the one, be as truly his Wrath and Rage burning in them, as the Light and Joy and Glory of the other, is only his Goodness opened and manifested in them, according to their *State in Nature*?

[Love-2.1-92] Take notice of this fundamental Truth.

[Love-2.1-93] Every Thing that works in Nature and Creature, except Sin, is the working of God in Nature and Creature. The Creature has nothing else in its Power but the free Use of its Will; and its free Will hath no other Power, but that of concurring with, or resisting the Working of God in Nature. The Creature with its free Will can bring nothing into Being, nor make any Alteration in the working of Nature, it can only change its *own State* or Place in the working of Nature, and so feel and find *something* in its State, that it did not feel or find before.

[Love-2.1-94] Thus God, in the *Manifestation* of himself in and by *Nature,* sets before every Man *Fire* and *Water, Life* and *Death*; and Man has no other Power, but that of entering into and uniting with either of these States, but not the least Power of adding to, or taking any Thing from them, or of making them to be otherwise than he finds them.

[Love-2.1-95] For this Fire and Water, this Life and Death, are *Nature*, and have their unchangeable State in the *uniform Working* of God in Nature. And therefore, whatever is done by this Fire and Water, this Life and Death in any Creature, may, nay, must, in the strictest Truth, be affirmed of God as done by Him. And consequently, every breathing forth of Fire, or Death, or Rage, or Curse, wherever it is, or in whatever Creature, must be said, in the Language of Scripture, to be a *provoked Wrath*, or *fiery Vengeance of God, poured forth upon the Creature*. And yet, every Thing that has been said in Proof of the Wrath of God shows, and proves to you at the same Time, that it is not a Wrath in the Holy Deity itself.

[Love-2.1-96] For you see, as was said above, that God sets before Man *Fire* and *Water*, *Life* and *Death*; now these Things are not God, nor existent in the Deity itself; but they are that which is, and is called *Nature*, and as they are the only Things set before Man, so Man can go no further, reach no further, nor find, nor feel, nor be sensible of any Thing else, but that which is to be felt or found in this *Nature*, or Fire and Water, Life and Death, which are set before him. And therefore all that Man can find or feel of the Wrath and Vengeance of God, can only be in *this Fire* and *this Death*, and not in the Deity itself.

[Love-2.1-97] *Theogenes.* Oh *Theophilus*, you have given me the utmost Satisfaction on this Point, and in a much better Way than I imagined. I expected to have seen you glossing and criticizing away the literal Expression of Scriptures that affirm the Wrath of God, in order to make good your Point, that the Deity is mere Love.

[Love-2.1-98] But you have done the utmost Justice to the *Letter* of Scripture, you have established it upon a firm and solid Foundation, and shown that the Truth of Things require it to be so, and that there can be no Wrath *anywhere*, but what is and must be called the Wrath and Vengeance of God, and yet is only in *Nature*.

[Love-2.1-99] What you have here said, seems as if it would clear up many Passages of Scripture that have raised much Perplexity. Methinks I begin to see how the *Hardness of Pharaoh's* Heart, how *Eyes* that see not, and *Ears* that hear not, may, in the strictest Truth, be said to be *of* or *from* God, though the Deity, in itself, stands in the utmost Contrariety to all these Things, and in the utmost Impossibility of *willing* or *causing* them to be.

[Love-2.1-100] But I must not draw you from our present Matter. You have shown, from the Letter of Scripture, that nothing else is set before Man but Fire and Water, Life and Death; and therefore, no Possibility of Wrath or Love, Joy or Sorrow, Curse or Happiness to be found by Man, but in *this State* of Nature set before him, or into which at his Creation he is introduced as into a *Region of various Sensibilities,* where all that he finds or feels, is truly God's, but not God himself, who has his supernatural Residence above, and distinct from every Thing that is Nature, Fire or Water, Life or Death.

[Love-2.1-101] But give me Leave to mention one Word of a Difficulty that I yet have. You have proved that Wrath, Rage, Vengeance, &c., can only exist, or be found *in Nature,* and not in God; and yet you say, that Nature is nothing else but a Manifestation of the hidden, invisible Powers of God. But if so, must not that which is in Nature be also in God? How else could Nature be a Manifestation of God?

[Love-2.1-102] *Theophilus*. Nature is a true Manifestation of the hidden, invisible God. But you are to observe, that Nature, as it is *in itself*, in its *own State*, cannot have the least possible Spark, or Stirring of Wrath, or Curse, or Vengeance in it: But, on the contrary, is from Eternity to Eternity, a mere Infinity of heavenly Light, Love, Joy, and Glory; and thus it is a true Manifestation of the hidden Deity, and the greatest of Proofs that the Deity itself can have no Wrath in it, since Wrath only then begins to be in Nature, when Nature has lost its first State.

[Love-2.1-103] *Theogenes*. This is Answer enough. But now another Thing starts up in my Mind. For if the Deity in itself, in its supernatural State, is *mere Love*, and only a *Will* to all Goodness, and if Nature in itself is only a Manifestation of this Deity of Love in heavenly Light and Glory, if neither God nor Nature have, or can give forth Wrath, how then can *Fire* and *Water*, *Life* and *Death* be set before Man? What can they come from, or where can they exist, since God in himself is all Love; and Nature, which is the Kingdom of Heaven, is an Infinity of Joy, Blessing, and Happiness?

[Love-2.1-104] *Theophilus*. I will open to you all this Matter to the Bottom in as few Words as I can.

[Love-2.1-105] Before God began any Creation, or gave Birth to any Creature, He was only manifested, or known to himself in his own Glory and Majesty; there was nothing but Himself beholding Himself in his own Kingdom of Heaven, which was, and is, and ever will be, as unlimited as Himself.

[Love-2.1-106] Nature, as well as God, is and must be antecedent to all Creature. For as no *seeing* Eye could be created, unless there was antecedently to it, a *natural Visibility* of Things, so no Creature could come into a *Sensibility* of any natural Life, unless such a State of Nature was antecedent to it. For no Creature can begin to be in any *World* or *State* of Nature, but by being created out of that World, or State of Nature, into which it is brought to have its Life. For to live in any World, is the same Thing as for a Creature to have all that it is, and has, *in* and *from* that World. And, therefore, no Creature can come into any other Kind of Existence and Life, but such as can be had *out of* that World in which it is to live. Neither can there possibly be any other Difference between created Beings, whether animate or inanimate, but what arises from that out of which they were created. Seeing then, that before the Existence of the first Creatures, there was nothing but God and his Kingdom of Heaven, the first Creatures could receive no other Life but that which was in God, because there was nothing *living* but God, nor any *other Life* but his, nor could they exist in any other Place or outward State, but the Kingdom of Heaven, because there was none else in Existence; and therefore, the first Creatures must, of all Necessity, be Divine and heavenly, both in their inward Life and outward State.

[Love-2.1-107] *Theogenes*. Here then, *Theophilus*, comes my Question. Where is that *Fire* and *Water*, that *Life* and *Death*, that is set before the Creature? For as to these first Creatures, nothing is set before them, nothing is within them, or without them, but God and the Kingdom of Heaven.

[Love-2.1-108] *Theophilus*. You should not have said, There is nothing *within* them, but God and the Kingdom of Heaven. For that which is their own *creaturely Nature* within them, is not God, nor the Kingdom of Heaven.

[Love-2.1-109] It has been already proved to your Satisfaction, that no Creature can be Divine, good, and happy, but by having a *two-fold* Life united in it. And in this two-fold Life of the Creature, is Fire and Water, Life and Death unavoidably set before it. For as its Will worketh with either of these Lives, so will it find either Fire or Water, Life or Death. If its Will turneth from the Life of God, into the creaturely Life, then it enters into a Sensibility of that which is meant by Death and Fire, *viz.*, a wrathful Misery. But if the Will keeps steadily given up to the Deity, then it lives in Possession of that *Life* and *Water,* which was its first, and will be its everlasting heavenly Joy and Happiness.

[Love-2.1-110] But to explain this Matter something deeper to you, according to the *Mystery* of all Things opened by God in his chosen Instrument, *Jacob Behmen.*

[Love-2.1-111] You know we have often spoken of *eternal Nature*, that so sure as there is an eternal God, so sure is it, that there is an eternal Nature, as universal, as unlimited as God Himself, and everywhere working where God is, and therefore, everywhere equally existent, as being his Kingdom of Heaven, or outward Manifestation of the invisible Riches, Powers, and Glories of the Deity.

[Love-2.1-112] Before, or without Nature, the Deity is an entire hidden, shut up, unknown, and unknowable Abyss. For Nature is the only Ground, or Beginning of *something*; there is neither *this* nor *that*, no Ground for *Conception*, no Possibility of *Distinction* or *Difference*; there cannot be a Creature to *think*, nor any Thing to be *thought* upon, till Nature is in Existence. For all the Properties of Sensibility and sensible Life, every Mode and Manner of Existence, all Seeing, Hearing, Tasting, Smelling, Feeling, all Inclinations, Passions, and Sensations of Joy, Sorrow, Pain, Pleasure, *&c.*, are not in God, but in Nature. And therefore, God is not knowable, not a Thought can begin about Him, till He manifests himself in, and through, and by the Existence of Nature; that is, till there is *something* that can be seen, understood, distinguished, felt, *&c.*

[Love-2.1-113] And this *eternal Nature,* or the Out-Birth of the Deity, called the *Kingdom of Heaven, viz.,* an Infinity, or boundless Opening of the Properties, Powers, Wonders, and Glories of the hidden Deity, and this not *once done,* but ever doing, ever standing in the *same Birth,* for ever and ever breaking forth and springing up in new Forms and Openings of the abyssal Deity, in the Powers of Nature. And out of this Ocean of manifested Powers of Nature, the Will of the Deity, created Hosts of heavenly Beings, full of the heavenly Wonders introduced into a Participation of the Infinity of God, to live in an eternal Succession of heavenly Sensations, to see and feel, to taste and find new Forms of Delight in an inexhaustible Source of ever-changing and never-ceasing Wonders of the Divine Glory.

[Love-2.1-114] Oh *Theogenes*! What an Eternity is this, out of which, and for which thy eternal Soul was created? What little, crawling Things are all that an earthly Ambition can set before Thee? Bear with Patience for a while the Rags of thy earthly Nature, the Veil and Darkness of Flesh and Blood, as the Lot of thy Inheritance from Father *Adam*, but think nothing worth a

Thought, but that which will bring thee back to thy first Glory, and land thee safe in the Region of Eternity.

[Love-2.1-115] But to return. Nothing is before this eternal Nature, but the holy, supernatural Deity; and every Thing that is after it, is *Creature*, and has all its creaturely Life and State in it, and from it, either mediately or immediately.

[Love-2.1-116] This eternal Nature hath seven *chief* or *fountain* Properties, that are the Doers, or Workers of every Thing that is done in it, and can have neither more nor less, because it is a Birth from, or a Manifestation of the Deity in Nature. For the Perfection of Nature (as was before said of every Divine and happy Creature) is an Union of *two Things*, or is a *two-fold State*. It is Nature, and it is God manifested in Nature. Now God is Triune, and Nature is Triune, and hence there arises the Ground of Properties, three and three; and that which brings those three and three into Union, or manifests the Triune God in the Triune Nature, is another Property; so that the glorious Manifestation of the Deity in Nature can have neither more nor less than seven *chief* or fountain Properties from which every Thing that is known, found, and felt, in all the Universe of Nature, in all the Variety of Creatures either in Heaven or on Earth, hath its only Rise, or Cause, either mediately or immediately.

[Love-2.1-117] *Theogenes*. You say, *Theophilus*, that the Triune Deity is united or manifested in *Triune Nature*, and that thence comes the glorious Manifestation of God in seven heavenly Properties called the Kingdom of Heaven. But how does it appear that *this Nature*, antecedently to the Entrance of the Deity into it, is Triune? Or what is this Triune Nature, before God is supposed to be in Union with it?

[Love-2.1-118] *Theophilus*. It is barely a Desire. It neither is, nor has, nor can be any Thing else but a *Desire*. For Desire is the *only Thing* in which the Deity can work and manifest itself; for God can only come into *That* which *wants* and *desires* him.

[Love-2.1-119] The Deity is an infinite Plenitude, or Fullness of Riches and Powers, in and from itself; and it is only want and Desire, that is excluded from It, and can have no Existence in it. And here lies the true, immutable Distinction between God and Nature, and shows why neither can ever be changed into the other; it is because God is a universal all; and Nature or *Desire* is a universal want, *viz.*, to be filled with God.

[Love-2.1-120] Now as Nature can be nothing but a *Desire*, so nothing is in, or done in any natural Way, but as *Desire* does it, because Desire is the *All* of Nature. And, therefore, there is no Strength or Substance, no Power or Motion, no Cause or Effect in Nature, but what is in itself a *Desire,* or the Working and Effect of it.

[Love-2.1-121] This is the true Origin of *Attraction,* and all its Powers, in this material World. It gives Essence and Substance to all that is *Matter* and the Properties of Matter; it holds every Element in its created State; and not only Earth and Stones, but *Light* and *Air* and Motion are under its Dominion. From the Centre to the Circumference of this material System, every Motion, Separation, Union, Vegetation, or Corruption begins no sooner, goes on no further, than as *Attraction* Works.

[Love-2.1-122] Take away Attraction from this material System, and then it has all the Annihilation it can ever possibly have.

[Love-2.1-123] Whence now has Attraction this Nature?

[Love-2.1-124] It is solely from hence; because *all Nature* from its Eternity, hath been, is, and for ever can be only a Desire, and hath nothing in it but the Properties of Desire.

[Love-2.1-125] Now the essential, inseparable Properties of Desire are the *three,* and can be neither more nor less; and in this you have that *Tri-Unity* of Nature which you asked after, and in which the Triune Deity manifesteth itself. I shall not now prove these three Properties of the Desire, because I have done it at large, and plainly enough elsewhere. *{ Way to Divine Knowledge; Spirit of Love, Part I }*

[Love-2.1-126] But to go back now to your Question, Where, or how this *Fire* and *Water, &c.*, can be found, since God is all Love and Goodness, and his *Manifestation* in Nature is a mere Kingdom of Heaven. They are to be found in the *two-fold State* of Heaven, and the *two-fold State* of every heavenly Creature.

[Love-2.1-127] For seeing that the Perfection of Nature, and the Perfection of the intelligent Creature, consists in one and the *same two-fold State*, you have here the plainest Ground and Reason why and how every good and happy and new created Being, must of all Necessity, have Fire and Water, Life and Death set before it, or put into its Choice.

[Love-2.1-128] Because it has it in its Power to turn and give up its Will to either of these Lives, it can turn either to God, or Nature, and therefore must have Life and Death, Fire or Water in its Choice.

[Love-2.1-129] Now this two-fold Life, which makes the Perfection of Nature and Creature, is, in other Words, signified by the *seven* heavenly Properties of Nature; for when God is manifested in Nature, all its seven Properties are in a heavenly State.

[Love-2.1-130] But in these seven Properties, though all heavenly, lieth the Ground of Fire and Water, *&c.*, because a *Division* or *Separation* can be made in them by the Will of the Creature. For the three first Properties are as distinct from the four following ones, as God is distinct from *That* which *wants* God. And these three first Properties are the Essence or whole Being of that *Desire,* which is, and is called *Nature*, or that which *wants* God.

[Love-2.1-131] When, therefore, the Will of the Creature turns from God into *Nature*, it breaks, or looses the Union of the seven heavenly Properties; because Nature, as distinct from God, has only the three first Properties in it. And such a Creature, having broken or lost the Union of the seven Properties, is fallen into the *three first*, which is meant by *Fire* and *Death*. For when the first three Properties have lost God, or their Union with the four following ones, then they are *mere Nature*, which, in its whole Being, is nothing else but the Strength and Rage of Hunger, an Excess of Want, of Self-Torment, and Self-Vexation. Surely now, my friend, this Matter is enough explained.

[Love-2.1-132] *Theogenes*. Indeed, *Theophilus*, I am quite satisfied; for by this Account which you have given of the Ground of *Nature,* and its true and full Distinction from God, you have struck a most amazing Light into my Mind.

[Love-2.1-133] For if Nature is *mere Want,* and has nothing in it but a *Strength* of Want, generated from the three self-tormenting Properties of a *Desire,* if God is all Love, Joy, and Happiness, an infinite Plenitude of all Blessings, then the Limits and Bounds of Good and Evil, of Happiness and Misery, are made as visibly distinct and as certainly to be known, as the Difference between a Circle and a straight Line.

[Love-2.1-134] To live to *Desire*, that is, to *Nature*, is unavoidably entering into the Region of all Evil and Misery; because *Nature* has nothing else in it. But on the other Hand, to die to *Desire*, that is, to turn from *Nature* to God, is to be united with the infinite Source of all that is good, and blessed, and happy.

[Love-2.1-135] All that I wanted to know, is now cleared up in the greatest Plainness. And I have no Difficulty about those passages of Scripture, which speak of the Wrath, and Fury, and Vengeance of God. Wrath is *his*, just as all Nature is *his*, and yet God is *mere Love,* that only rules and governs Wrath, as He governs the foaming Waves of the Sea, and the Madness of Storms and Tempests.

[Love-2.1-136] The following Propositions are as evidently true, as that two and two are four.

[Love-2.1-137] *First*, That God in his holy Deity is as absolutely free from *Wrath* and *Rage,* and as utterly incapable of them as He is of *Thickness, Hardness,* and *Darkness;* because Wrath and Rage belong to nothing else, can exist in nothing else, have Life in nothing else, but in Thickness, Hardness, and Darkness.

[Love-2.1-138] *Secondly*, That all Wrath is Disorder, and can be nowhere but in Nature and Creature, because nothing else is capable of changing from Right to Wrong.

[Love-2.1-139] *Thirdly*, That Wrath can have no Existence even in Nature and Creature, till they have lost their first Perfection which they had from God, and are become *that* which they should not have been.

[Love-2.1-140] *Fourthly*, That all the Wrath, and Fury, and Vengeance, that ever did, or can break forth in Nature and Creature is, according to the strictest Truth, to be called and looked upon as the Wrath and Vengeance of God, just as the *Darkness,* as well as the *Light* is, and is to be called his.

[Love-2.1-141] Oh! *Theophilus*, what a Key have you given me to the right understanding of Scripture!

[Love-2.1-142] For when Nature and Creature are known to be the *only Theater* of Evil and Disorder, and the holy Deity as that governing Love, which wills nothing but the Removal of all Evil from every Thing, as fast as infinite Wisdom can find Ways of doing it, then whether you read of the raining of *Fire* and *Brimstone,* or only Showers of *heavenly Manna* falling upon the Earth, it is only one and the *same Love,* working in such different Ways and Diversity of Instruments, as *Time,* and *Place,* and *Occasion,* had made wise, and good, and beneficial.

[Love-2.1-143] *Pharaoh* with his hardened Heart, and St *Paul* with his Voice from Heaven, though so contrary to one another, were both of them the chosen Vessels of the same God of Love, because both miraculously taken out of their *own State,* and made to do all the Good to a blind and wicked World, which they were capable of doing.

[Love-2.1-144] And thus, Sir, are all the Treasures of the Wisdom and Goodness of God, hidden in the Letter of Scripture, made the Comfort and Delight of my Soul, and every Thing I read turns itself into a Motive, of loving and adoring the wonderful Working of the Love of God over all the various Changings of Nature and Creature, till all Evil shall be extinguished, and all Disorder go back again to its first harmonious State of Perfection.

[Love-2.1-145] Depart from this Idea of God, as an *Infinity of mere Love, Wisdom,* and *Goodness,* and then every Thing in the System of Scripture, and the System of Nature, only helps the reasoning Mind to be miserably perplexed, as well with the Mercies, as with the Judgments of God.

[Love-2.1-146] But when God is known to be *omnipotent Love,* that can do nothing but *Works of Love,* and that all Nature and Creature are only under the Operation of Love, as a distempered Person under the Care of a kind and skillful Physician, who seeks nothing but the perfect Recovery of his Patient, then whatever is done, whether a severe *Caustic,* or a pleasant *Cordial* is ordered, that is, whether because of its Difference, it may have the different Name of *Mercy* or *Judgment,* yet all is equally well done, because Love is the *only Doer* of both, and does both, from the same Principle, and for the same End.

[Love-2.1-147] *Theophilus.* Oh *Theogenes,* Now you are according to your Name, you are born of God. For when Love is the Triune God that you serve, worship, and adore, the only God, in whom you desire to live and move and have your Being, then of a Truth God dwelleth in you, and you in God.

[Love-2.1-148] I shall now only add this one Word more, to strengthen and confirm your right understanding of all that is said of the Wrath, or Rage of God in the Scriptures.

[Love-2.1-149] The Psalmist, you know, saith thus of God, "He giveth forth *his Ice* like Morsels, and who is able to abide *his Frosts?*" Now, Sir, if you know how to explain this Scripture, and can show how *Ice* and *Frost* can truly be ascribed to God, *as His,* though absolutely impossible to have any Existence in Him, then you have an easy and unerring Key, how the Wrath, and Fury, and Vengeance, that anywhere falls upon any Creature is, and may be truly ascribed to God, *as his,* though Fury and Vengeance are as inconsistent with, and as impossible to have any Existence in the Deity, as lumps of Ice, or the Hardness of intolerable Frosts.

[Love-2.1-150] Now in this Text, setting forth the Horror of God's *Ice* and *Frost,* you have the whole Nature of Divine Wrath set before you. Search all the Scriptures, and you will nowhere find any Wrath of God, but what is bounded in *Nature*, and is so described, as to be itself a Proof, that it has no Existence in the holy supernatural Deity.

[Love-2.1-151] Thus says the Psalmist again, "The Earth trembled and quaked, the very Foundations also of the Hills shook, and were removed, because he was wroth." No Wrath here but in the Elements.

[Love-2.1-152] Again, "There went a Smoke out in his Presence, and a consuming Fire out of his Mouth, so that Coals were kindled at it. The Springs of Water were seen, and the Foundations of the round World were discovered at thy chiding, O Lord, at the blasting of the Breath of thy Displeasure."

[Love-2.1-153] Now every Working of the Wrath of God, described in Scripture, is strictly of a Piece with this, it relates to a Wrath solely confined to the Powers and working Properties of Nature, that lives and moves only in the Elements of the fallen World, and no more reaches the Deity, than *Ice* or *Frost* do.

[Love-2.1-154] The Apostle saith, "Avenge not yourselves, for it is written, Vengeance is mine, I Will repay, saith the Lord."

[Love-2.1-155] This is another full Proof, that Wrath or Vengeance is not in the holy Deity itself, as a Quality of the Divine Mind; for if it was, then Vengeance would belong to every Child of God, that was truly born of Him, or he could not have the Spirit of his Father, or be perfect as his Father in Heaven is perfect.

[Love-2.1-156] But if Vengeance only belongs to God, and can only be so affirmed of Him, as Ice and Frost are *His*, and belong to Him, if it has no other Manner of Working, than as when it is said, "He sent out his Arrows and scattered them, He cast forth Lightnings and destroyed them"; then it is certain, that the Divine Vengeance is only in *fallen Nature,* and its *disordered Properties,* and is no more in the Deity itself, than *Hailstones* and *Coals* of Fire.

[Love-2.1-157] And here you have the true Reason, why Revenge or Vengeance is not allowed to Man; it is because Vengeance can only work in the evil, or disordered Properties of *fallen Nature*. But Man being Himself a *Part* of fallen Nature, and *subject* to its disordered Properties, is not allowed to work with them, because it would be stirring up Evil in himself, and that is his Sin of Wrath, or Revenge.

[Love-2.1-158] God therefore reserves all Vengeance to Himself, not because wrathful Revenge is a Temper or Quality that can have any Place in the Holy Deity, but because the holy supernatural Deity, being free from all the Properties of Nature, whence partial Love and Hatred spring, and being in Himself nothing but an Infinity of Love, Wisdom, and Goodness, He alone knows how to over-rule the Disorders of Nature, and so to repay Evil with Evil, that the highest good may be promoted by it.

[Love-2.1-159] To say, therefore, that Vengeance is to be reserved to God, is only saying in other Words, that all the Evils in Nature are to be reserved and turned over to the *Love* of God, to be healed by his *Goodness*. And every Act of what is called Divine Vengeance, recorded in Scripture, may, and ought, with the greatest strictness of Truth, be called an Act of the Divine Love.

[Love-2.1-160] If *Sodom* flames and smokes with stinking Brimstone, it is the Love of God that kindled it, only to extinguish a *more horrible Fire*. It was one and the same infinite Love, when it preserved *Noah* in the Ark, when it turned *Sodom* into a burning Lake, and overwhelmed *Pharaoh* in the Red Sea. And if God commanded the Waters to destroy the old World, it was as high an Act of the same infinite Love toward *that Chaos,* as when it said to the first Darkness upon the Face of the Deep, "Let there be Light, and there was Light."

[Love-2.1-161] Not a Word in all Scripture concerning the Wrath or Vengeance of God but directly teaches you these two infallible truths. First, that all the Wrath spoken of worketh nowhere but in the wrathful, disordered Elements and Properties of fallen Nature. Secondly, that all the Power that God exercises over them, all that he doth at any Time or on any Occasion with or by them is only and solely the one Work of his unchangeable Love toward Man.

[Love-2.1-162] Just as the good *Physician* acts from only one and the same *good Will* toward his Patient, when he orders bitter and sour, as when he gives the pleasant Draughts.

[Love-2.1-163] Now, suppose the good Physician to have such intense Love for you, as to disregard your Aversion toward them, and to force such Medicines down your Throat, as can alone save your Life; suppose he should therefore call himself your *severe* Physician, and declare himself *so rigid* toward you, that he would *not spare* you, nor *suffer* you, go where you would, to *escape* his bitter Draughts, till all Means of your Recovery were tried, then you would have a true and just, though low Representation of those bitter Cups, which God in *his Wrath* forceth fallen Man to drink.

[Love-2.1-164] Now as the bitter, *sour, hot, &c.*, in the Physician's Draughts, are not Declarations of any the like Bitterness, Heat, or Sourness in the *Spirit* of the Physician that uses them, but are Things quite distinct from the *State* and *Spirit* of his Mind, and only manifest his *Care* and *Skill* in the right Use of *such Materials* toward the Health of his Patient; so in like Manner, all the Elements of fallen Nature are only so many *outward Materials* in the Hands of God, formed and mixed into Heat and Cold, into fruitful and pestilential Effects, into Serenity of Seasons, and blasting Tempests, into Means of Health and Sickness, of Plenty and Poverty, just as the Wisdom and Goodness of Providence sees to be the fittest to deliver Man from the miserable Malady of his earthly Nature and help him to become heavenly-minded.

[Love-2.1-165] If, therefore, it would be great Folly to suppose *Bitterness*, or Heat, *&c.*, to be in the Spirit of the Physician, when he gives a hot or bitter Medicine, much greater Folly surely must it be, to suppose that Wrath, Vengeance, or any pestilential Quality, is in the Spirit of the holy Deity, when a Wrath, a Vengeance, or Pestilence is stirred up in the fallen Elements by the Providence of God, as a proper Remedy for the Evil of this, or that Time or Occasion.

[Love-2.1-166] Hear these decisive words of Scripture, *viz.,* "Whom the Lord loveth, he chasteneth." What a Grossness therefore of Mistake is it to conclude, that Wrath must be in the

Deity, because He chastens and threatens Chastisement, when you have God's own Word for it, that nothing but his Love chasteneth? Again, Thus saith the Lord, "I have smitten you with Blasting and Mildew. Your Vineyards, and your Fig Trees, and your Olive Yards, did the Palmer-Worm devour," and then the Love that did this makes this Complaint, "Yet ye have not returned to me." Again, "Pestilence have I sent amongst you; I have made the Stink of your Tents come up even into your Nostrils," &c. And then the same Love that did this, that made this Use of the disordered Elements, makes the same Complaint again, "Yet have ye not returned to me" (Amos 4:9-10).

[Love-2.1-167] Now, Sir, How is it possible for Words to give stronger Proof, that God is mere Love, that he has no Will toward fallen Man but to bless him with Works of Love, and this as certainly, when he turns the Air into a *Pestilence,* as when he makes the same Air rain down *Manna* upon the Earth, since neither the one nor the other are done, but as Time, and Place, and Occasion, render them the fittest Means to make Man return and adhere to God, that is, to come out of all the Evil and Misery of his fallen State? What can infinite Love do more, or what can it do to give greater Proof, that all that it does proceeds from Love? And here you are to observe, that this is not said from human Conjecture, or any imaginary Idea of God, but is openly asserted, constantly affirmed, and repeated in the plainest Letter of Scripture. But this Conversation has been long enough. And I hope we shall meet again To-morrow.

The Second Dialogue between Theogenes, Eusebius, and Theophilus

[Love-2.2-1] *EUSEBIUS.* There is no Occasion to resume any Thing of our Yesterday's Discourse. The following Propositions are sufficiently proved.

[Love-2.2-2] *First,* That God is an abyssal Infinity of Love, Wisdom, and Goodness; that He ever was, and ever will be one and the same unchangeable *Will to all Goodness and Works of Love,* as incapable of any *Sensibility* of Wrath, or acting under it, as of falling into Pain or Darkness, and acting under their Direction.

[Love-2.2-3] *Secondly,* That all Wrath, Strife, Discord, Hatred, Envy, or Pride, &c., all Heat and Cold, all Enmity in the Elements, all Thickness, Grossness, and Darkness are Things that have no Existence but in and from the Sphere of fallen Nature.

[Love-2.2-4] *Thirdly,* That all the Evils of Contrariety and Disorder in fallen Nature are only as so many Materials in the Hands of infinite Love and Wisdom, all made to work in their different Ways, as far as is possible, to one and the same End, *viz.,* to turn temporal Evil into eternal Good.

[Love-2.2-5] So that whether you look at Light or Darkness, at Night or Day, at Fire or Water, at Heaven or Earth, at Life or Death, at Prosperity or Adversity, at blasting Winds or heavenly Dews, at Sickness or Health, you see nothing but *such a State* of Things, in and through which, the *supernatural* Deity *wills* and *seeks* the Restoration of fallen Nature and Creature to their first Perfection.

[Love-2.2-6] It now only remains, that the Doctrine of Scripture concerning the *Atonement,* necessary to be made by the Life, Sufferings, and Death of Christ be explained, or in other Words, the true Meaning of that *Righteousness* or *Justice* of God, that must have Satisfaction done to it, before Man can be reconciled to God.

[Love-2.2-7] For this Doctrine is thought by some to favour the Opinion of a *Wrath* and Resentment in the Deity itself.

[Love-2.2-8] *Theophilus.* This Doctrine, *Eusebius,* of the Atonement made by Christ, and the absolute Necessity and real Efficacy of it, to *satisfy* the Righteousness, or Justice of God, is the very Ground and Foundation of Christian Redemption, and the Life and Strength of every Part of it. But then, this very Doctrine is so far from favouring the Opinion of a Wrath in the Deity itself, that it is an absolute full Denial of it, and the strongest of Demonstrations, that the Wrath, or Resentment, that is to be pacified or atoned, cannot possibly be in the Deity itself.

[Love-2.2-9] For this Wrath that is to be *atoned* and *pacified* is, in its whole Nature, nothing else but *Sin,* or *Disorder* in the Creature. And when Sin is *extinguished* in the Creature, all the Wrath that is *between* God and the Creature is *fully atoned.* Search all the Bible, from one End to the other, and you will find, that the Atonement of *that* which is called the Divine Wrath or Justice, and the *extinguishing* of Sin in the Creature, are only different Expressions for *one and the same* individual Thing. And therefore, unless you will place Sin in God, that Wrath, that is to be atoned or pacified, cannot be placed in Him.

[Love-2.2-10] The whole Nature of our Redemption has no other End, but to remove or extinguish the Wrath that is between God and Man. When this is removed, Man is *reconciled* to God. Therefore, *where* the Wrath is, or where *that* is which wants to be atoned, *there* is that which is the *blamable Cause* of the Separation between God and Man; *there* is that which Christ came into the World to extinguish, to quench, or atone. If, therefore, this Wrath, which is the *blamable Cause* of the Separation between God and Man, is in God Himself, if Christ died to atone, or extinguish a Wrath that was got into the holy Deity itself, then it must be said, that Christ made an Atonement for God, and not for Man; that He died for the Good and Benefit of God, and not of Man; and that which is called *our Redemption,* ought rather to be called the Redemption of God, as saving and delivering Him, and not Man, from his *own Wrath.*

[Love-2.2-11] This Blasphemy is unavoidable, if you suppose *that* Wrath, for which Christ died, to be a Wrath in God Himself.

[Love-2.2-12] *Again,* The very Nature of *Atonement* absolutely shows, that *that* which is to be atoned cannot possibly be in God, nor even in any good Being. For Atonement implies the *Alteration,* or Removal of something that is not as it ought to be. And therefore, every Creature, so long as it is good, and has its *proper State* of Goodness, neither wants, nor can admit of any Atonement, because it has nothing in it that wants to be *altered* or *taken out* of it. And therefore, Atonement cannot possibly have any Place in God, because nothing in God either wants, or can receive Alteration; neither can it have Place in any Creature, but so far as it has lost, or altered *that* which it had from God, and is fallen into Disorder; and then, that which brings this Creature back to its first State, which alters that which is wrong in it, and takes its Evil out of it, is its *true* and *proper Atonement*.

[Love-2.2-13] *Water* is the proper Atonement of the Rage of Fire; and that which *changes* a Tempest into a Calm is its true Atonement. And, therefore, as sure as Christ is a *Propitiation* and *Atonement*, so sure is it, that *that* which he does, as a Propitiation and Atonement, can have no Place, but in altering that Evil and Disorder which, in the State and Life of the fallen Creature, wants to be altered.

[Love-2.2-14] Suppose the Creature not fallen, and then there is no Room nor Possibility for Atonement; a plain and full Proof, that the Work of Atonement is nothing else but the altering or quenching that which is Evil in the fallen Creature.

[Love-2.2-15] *Hell, Wrath, Darkness, Misery*, and *eternal Death,* mean the same Thing through all Scripture, and these are the only Things from which we want to be redeemed; and where there is nothing of Hell, *there,* there is nothing of *Wrath*, nor any Thing that wants, or can admit of the Benefits of the Atonement made by Christ.

[Love-2.2-16] Either, therefore, all Hell is in the Essence of the holy Deity, or nothing that wants to be atoned by the Merits and Death of Christ, can possibly be in the Deity itself.

[Love-2.2-17] The Apostle saith, that "we are by Nature Children of Wrath"; the same Thing as when the Psalmist saith, "I was shapen in Wickedness, and in Sin hath my Mother conceived me." And therefore, that Wrath which *wants* the Atonement of the Sufferings, Blood, and Death of Christ, is no other than that *Sin,* or *sinful State,* in which we are naturally born. But now, if this *Wrath* could be supposed to be in the Deity itself, then it would follow, that by *being by Nature Children of Wrath*, we should thereby be the *true Children* of God; we should not want any Atonement, or new Birth from above, to make us *Partakers of the Divine Nature,* because that Wrath that was in us would be our dwelling in God and he in us.

[Love-2.2-18] *Again,* All Scripture teaches us, That God *wills* and desires the Removal, or Extinction of *that Wrath,* which is *betwixt* God and the Creature; and therefore, all Scripture teaches, that the Wrath is not in God; for God cannot will the Removal, or Alteration of any Thing that is in Himself; this is as impossible, as for him to *will* the Extinction of his own Omnipotence. Nor can there be any Thing in God, contrary to, or against his own Will; and yet, if God *wills* the Extinction of a Wrath that is in Himself, it must be in Him, contrary to, or against his own Will.

[Love-2.2-19] This, I presume, is enough to show you, that the Atonement made by Christ is itself the greatest of all Proofs, that it was not to atone or extinguish any Wrath in the Deity itself; nor, indeed, any Way to affect, or alter any Quality, or Temper in the Divine Mind, but purely and solely to overcome and remove all that Death and Hell, and Wrath, and Darkness, that had opened itself in the Nature, Birth, and Life of fallen Man.

[Love-2.2-20] *Eusebius.* The Truth of all this is not to be denied. And yet it is as true, that all our Systems of Divinity give quite another Account of this most important Matter. The *Satisfaction* of Christ is represented as a Satisfaction made to a wrathful Deity; and the Merits of the Sufferings and Death of Christ, as *that* which could only avail with God, to give up his *own Wrath,* and think of Mercy toward Man. Nay, what is still worse, if possible, the Ground, and Nature, and Efficacy of this great Transaction between God and Man, is often explained by *Debtor* and *Creditor*: Man, as having contracted a Debt with God that he could not pay, and God, as having a Right to insist upon the Payment of it; and therefore, only to be satisfied by receiving the Death and Sacrifice of Christ, as a valuable Consideration, instead of the Debt that was due to Him from Man.

[Love-2.2-21] *Theophilus.* Hence you may see, *Eusebius,* how unreasonably Complaint has been sometimes made against the *Appeal,* the *Spirit of Prayer, &c.*, as introducing a Philosophy into the Doctrines of the Gospel, not enough supported by the Letter of Scripture; though every Thing there asserted has been over and over shown to be well grounded on the Letter of Scripture, and necessarily included in the most fundamental Doctrines of the Gospel.

[Love-2.2-22] Yet they who make this Complaint, blindly swallow a Vanity of Philosophy, in the most important part of Gospel Religion, which not only has less Scripture for it than the Infallibility of the Pope, but is directly contrary to the plain Letter of every single Text of Scripture that relates to this Matter: as I will now show you.

[Love-2.2-23] *First,* The Apostle saith, "God so loved the World, that he gave his only begotten Son, that all who believe in Him should not perish but have everlasting Life." What becomes now of the Philosophy of *Debtor* and *Creditor*, of a Satisfaction made by Christ to a Wrath in God? Is it not the grossest of all Fictions, and in full Contrariety to the plain written Word of God? "God so loved the World"; behold the Degree of it? But when did He so love it? Why, before it was redeemed, before He sent or gave his only Son to be the Redeemer of it. Here you see, that all Wrath *in God, antecedent* to our Redemption, or the Sacrifice of Christ for us, is utterly excluded; there is no Possibility for the Supposition of it, it is as absolutely denied as Words can do it. And therefore the infinite Love, Mercy, and Compassion of God toward fallen Man, are not *purchased,* or *procured* for us by the Death of Christ, but the Incarnation and Sufferings of Christ come from, and are given to us by the infinite *antecedent* Love of God for us, and are the gracious Effects of his own Love and Goodness toward us.

[Love-2.2-24] It is needless to show you, how constantly this same Doctrine is asserted and repeated by all the Apostles.

[Love-2.2-25] Thus says St. John again, "In this was manifested the Love of God toward us, because he sent his only begotten Son into the World, that we might live through him." Again, "this is the Record, that God hath given unto us eternal Life; and this Life is in his Son." Again, "God," saith St. Paul, "was in Christ, reconciling the World unto Himself, not imputing their Trespasses to them." Which is repeated, and further opened in these Words, "Giving Thanks unto the Father, who hath made us meet to be Partakers of the Inheritance of the Saints in Light, who hath delivered us from the Power of Darkness, and hath translated us into the Kingdom of his dear Son" (Col. 1:12-13). And again, "Blessed be the God and Father of our Lord Jesus Christ, who hath blessed us with all spiritual Blessings in heavenly Places in Christ" (Eph. 1:3).

[Love-2.2-26] How great therefore, *Eusebius*, is the Error, how total the Disregard of Scripture, and how vain the Philosophy, which talks of a Wrath in God *antecedent* to our Redemption, or of a Debt which he could not forgive us, till he had received a *Valuable Consideration* for it, when all Scriptures from Page to Page tells us, that all the Mercy and Blessing and Benefits of Christ, as our Saviour, are the *free antecedent* Gift of God Himself to us, and bestowed upon us for no other Reason, from no other Motive, but the Infinity of his own Love toward us, agreeable to what the Evangelical Prophet saith of God, "I am He that blotteth out Transgressions for my own sake" (Isa. 43:25), that is, not for any Reason or Motive that can be laid before me but because I am Love itself, and my own Nature is my immutable Reason why nothing but Works of Love, Blessing, and Goodness, can come from me.

[Love-2.2-27] Look we now at the Scripture Account of the Nature of the Atonement and Satisfaction of Christ, and this will further show us, that it is not to atone, or alter any *Quality* or *Temper* in the Divine Mind, nor for the Sake of God, but purely and solely to atone, to quench, and overcome that Death, and Wrath, and Hell, under the Power of which Man was fallen.

[Love-2.2-28] "As in Adam all die, so in Christ shall all be made alive." This is the whole *Work*, the whole *Nature*, and the sole *End* of Christ's Sacrifice of Himself; and there is not a Syllable in Scripture, that gives you any other account of it. It all consists, from the Beginning to the End, in carrying on the one Work of *Regeneration*; and therefore the Apostle saith, "The first Adam was made a living Soul, but the last or Second Adam was made a Quickening Spirit," because sent into the World by God to quicken and revive that Life from above which we lost in *Adam*. And he is called our *Ransom*, our *Atonement*, &c., for no other Reason, but because that which He did and suffered in our fallen Nature, was as truly an *efficacious Means* of our being born again to a new heavenly Life, of Him, and from Him, as that which *Adam* did, was the *true* and *natural Cause* of our being born in Sin, and the Impurity of bestial Flesh and Blood.

[Love-2.2-29] And as *Adam,* by what He did, may be truly said to have *purchased* our Misery and Corruption, to have *bought* Death for us, and to have *sold* us into a Slavery under the World, the Flesh, and the Devil, though all that we have from him, or suffer by him, is only the *inward working of his own Nature and Life within us*, so, according to the plain meaning of the Words, Christ may be said to be our *Price*, our *Ransom*, and *Atonement*; though all that He does for us, as Buying, Ransoming, and Redeeming us, is done wholly and solely by a Birth of his *own Nature and Spirit* brought to Life in us.

[Love-2.2-30] The apostle saith, "Christ died for our Sins." Thence it is, that He is the great Sacrifice for Sin and its true Atonement. But how and why is he so? The Apostle tells you in these Words, "The Sting of Death is Sin;— but Thanks be to God, who giveth us the Victory through our Lord Jesus Christ"; and therefore Christ is the Atonement of our Sins when, by and from Him, living in us, we have Victory over our sinful Nature.

[Love-2.2-31] The Scriptures frequently say, Christ *gave himself for us*. But what is the full Meaning, Effect, and Benefit, of his thus *giving Himself for us*? The Apostle puts this out of all

Doubt, when he says, "Jesus Christ, who gave Himself for us, that He might redeem us from all Iniquity, and purify to Himself a peculiar People;—that He might deliver us from this present World,—from the Curse of the Law,—from the Power of Satan,— from the Wrath to come"; or as the Apostle saith in other Words, "that He might be made unto us, Wisdom, Righteousness, and Sanctification."

[Love-2.2-32] The whole Truth therefore of the Matter is plainly this. Christ given *for us*, is neither more nor less, than Christ given *into us*. And he is in no other Sense, our full, perfect, and sufficient Atonement, than as his Nature and Spirit are born, and formed in us, which so purgeth us from our Sins, that we are thereby in Him, and by Him dwelling in us, become new Creatures, having our Conversation in Heaven.

[Love-2.2-33] As *Adam* is truly our *Defilement* and *Impurity*, by his Birth in us, so Christ is our *Atonement* and *Purification*, by our being born again of Him, and having thereby quickened and revived in us that first Divine Life, which was extinguished in *Adam*. And therefore, as *Adam purchased* Death for us, just so in the same Manner, in the same Degree, and in the same Sense, Christ *purchases* Life for us. And each of them only, and solely by their *own inward Life* within us.

[Love-2.2-34] This is the one Scripture Account of the whole Nature, the sole End, and full Efficacy of all that Christ did, and suffered for us. It is all comprehended in these two Texts of Scripture: (1) "That Christ was manifested to destroy the Works of the Devil; (2) That as in Adam all die, so in Christ shall all be made alive." From the Beginning to the End of Christ's atoning Work, no other Power is ascribed to it, nothing else is intended by it, as an *Appeaser* of Wrath, but the destroying of all that in Man which comes from the Devil; no other *Merits*, or *Value*, or infinite *Worth*, than that of its infinite Ability, and Sufficiency to *quicken again* in all human Nature, that Heavenly Life that died in *Adam*.

[Love-2.2-35] *Eusebius*. Though all that is here said seems to have both the Letter and the Spirit of Scripture on its Side, yet I am afraid it will be thought not enough to assert the infinite Value and Merits of our Saviour's Sufferings. For it is the common Opinion of Doctors that the Righteousness or Justice of God must have Satisfaction done to it; And that nothing could avail with God, as a Satisfaction, but the infinite Worth and Value of the Sufferings of Christ.

[Love-2.2-36] *Theophilus*. It is true, *Eusebius*, that this is often, and almost always thus asserted in human Writers, but it is neither the Language nor the Doctrine of Scripture.

[Love-2.2-37] Not a Word is there said of a Righteousness or Justice as an *Attribute in God*, that must be satisfied; or that the Sacrifice of Christ, is that which satisfies the Righteousness that is in God Himself.

[Love-2.2-38] It has been sufficiently proved to you, that God wanted not to be reconciled to fallen Man; that He never was anything else toward him but Love; and that his Love brought forth the whole Scheme of his Redemption. Thence it is, that the Scriptures do not say that Christ came into the World to procure us the Divine Favour and good Will, in order to put a Stop to *antecedent* righteous Wrath in God toward us. No, the Reverse of all this is the Truth, *viz.*, that

Christ and his whole mediatorial Office came *purely* and *solely* from God, already so reconciled to us, as to bestow an Infinity of Love upon us. "The God of all Grace," saith the Apostle, "who hath called us to his eternal Glory by Jesus Christ" (1 Pet. 5:10). Here you see, Christ is not the *Cause* or *Motive* of God's Mercy toward fallen Man, but God's *own Love* for us, his *own Desire* of our eternal Glory and Happiness hath for that End given us Christ, that we may be made Partakers of it. The same as when it is again said, "God was in Christ reconciling the World to Himself," that is, calling, and raising it out of its ungodly and miserable State.

[Love-2.2-39] Thus all the Mystery of our Redemption proclaims nothing but a God of Love toward fallen Man. It was the Love of God, that could not behold the Misery of fallen Man, without demanding and calling for his Salvation. It was Love alone, that wanted to have *full Satisfaction* done to it, and such a Love as could not be *satisfied,* till all that Glory and Happiness that was lost by the Death of *Adam,* was fully restored and regained again by the Death of Christ.

[Love-2.2-40] *Eusebius.* But is there not some good Sense, in which Righteousness or Justice may be said to be *satisfied* by the Atonement and Sacrifice of Christ?

[Love-2.2-41] *Theophilus.* Yes, most certainly there is. But then it is only *that* Righteousness or Justice that *belongs* to Man, and ought to be *in him.* Now Righteousness, wherever it is to be, has *no Mercy* in itself; it makes *no Condescensions*; it is *inflexibly* rigid; its Demands are *inexorable*; Prayers, Offerings, and Entreaties have *no Effect* upon it; it will have nothing but itself, nor will it ever cease its Demands, or take any Thing *in lieu* of them, as a Satisfaction instead of itself. Thus, "Without Holiness," saith the Apostle, "no Man shall see the Lord." And again, "Nothing that is defiled, or impure, can enter into the Kingdom of Heaven." And this is meant by Righteousness being *rigid* and having no *Mercy*; it cannot *spare*, or have *Pity*, or hear Entreaty, because all its Demands are righteous, and good, and therefore must be satisfied, or fulfilled.

[Love-2.2-42] Now Righteousness has its *absolute Demands* upon Man, because Man was created *righteous,* and has lost that *original* Righteousness, which he ought to have kept in its first Purity. And this is the *one, only Righteousness,* or Justice, which Christ came into the World to *satisfy,* not by giving some highly valuable Thing as a Satisfaction to it, but by bringing back, or raising up again in all human Nature, that Holiness or Righteousness, which originally *belonged* to it. For to *satisfy* Righteousness, means neither more nor less than to *fulfill* it. Nor can Righteousness *want* to have Satisfaction in any Being, but in that Being, which has *fallen* from it; nor can it be satisfied, but in restoring or fulfilling Righteousness in that Being, which had departed from it. And therefore the Apostle saith, that "we are created again unto Righteousness in Christ Jesus." And this is the *one* and *only* Way of Christ's expiating, or taking away the Sins of the World, namely, by restoring to Man his *lost* Righteousness. For this End, saith the Scripture, "Christ gave Himself for the Church, that He might sanctify and cleanse it, that he might present it to Himself a glorious Church, not having Spot, or Wrinkle, or any such Thing, but that it should be holy and without Blemish" (Eph. 5:25-27).

[Love-2.2-43] This is the one Righteousness, which Christ came into the World to satisfy, by fulfilling it himself, and enabling Man by a new Birth from him to fulfill it. And when all Unrighteousness is removed by Christ from the whole human Nature, then all that Righteousness is satisfied, for the doing of which, Christ poured out his most precious, availing, and meritorious Blood.

[Love-2.2-44] *Eusebius*. Oh *Theophilus*, the Ground on which you stand must certainly be true. It so easily, so fully solves all Difficulties and Objections, and enables you to give so plain and solid an Account of every Part of our Redemption. This great Point is so fully cleared up to me, that I do not desire another Word about it.

[Love-2.2-45] *Theophilus*. However, *Eusebius*, I will add a Word or two more upon it, that there may be no Room left, either for misunderstanding, or denying what has been just now said of the Nature of that Righteousness, which must have *full Satisfaction* done to it by the Atoning and Redeeming Work of Christ. And then you will be fully possessed of these two great Truths. *First*, That there is no righteous Wrath in the Deity itself, and therefore none to be atoned there. *Secondly*, That though God is in Himself a mere Infinity of Love, from whom nothing else but Works of Love and Blessing and Goodness can proceed, yet sinful Men are hereby not at all delivered from *That* which the Apostle calls the *Terrors of the Lord*, but that all the *Threatenings* of *Woe, Misery*, and *Punishment,* denounced in Scripture against Sin and Sinners, both in this World, and that which is to come, stand all of them in their *full Force*, and are not in the least Degree *weakened*, or *less* to be dreaded because God is *all Love*.

[Love-2.2-46] Every Thing that God hath created, is right and just and good in its Kind, and hath its *own* Righteousness within itself. The Rectitude of its Nature is its *only Law*; and it hath no other Righteousness, but that of continuing in its first State. No Creature is subject to any Pain, or Punishment, or Guilt of Sin, but because it has departed from its *first right* State, and only does, and can feel the painful Loss of its own first Perfection. And every intelligent Creature, that departs from the State of its Creation, is *unrighteous*, evil, and full of its *own Misery*. And there is no Possibility for any disordered, fallen Creature to be free from its *own Misery* and *Pain,* till it is again in its first State of Perfection. This is the certain and infallible Ground of the absolute Necessity, either of a perfect Holiness in this Life, or of a *further Purification* after Death, before Man can enter into the Kingdom of Heaven.

[Love-2.2-47] Now this *Pain* and *Misery,* which is inseparable from the Creature that is not in that State in which it ought to be, and in which it was created, is nothing else but the painful State of the Creature for Want of its *own proper Righteousness*, as Sickness is the painful State of the Creature for Want of *its own proper Health.*

[Love-2.2-48] No *other* Righteousness, or other Justice, no *other* severe Vengeance, demands Satisfaction, or *torments* the Sinner, but that very Righteousness, which once was *in him*, which still *belongs* to him, and therefore will not suffer him to have any Rest or Peace, till it is again in him as it was at the first. All, therefore, that Christ does as an *Atonement* for Sin, or as a Satisfaction to Righteousness, is all done in, and to, and for Man, and has no other Operation but that of *renewing* the fallen Nature of Man, and *raising* it up into its first State of *original Righteousness*. And if this Righteousness, which belongs solely to Man, and wants no Satisfaction, but that of being *restored* and *fulfilled* in the human Nature, is sometimes called the Righteousness of God, it is only so called, because it is a Righteousness which Man had originally from God, in and by his Creation; and, therefore, as it comes from God, has its whole

Nature and Power of Working as it does from God, it may very justly be called God's Righteousness.

[Love-2.2-49] Agreeably to this Way of ascribing that to God, which is only in the *State* and *Condition* of Man, the Psalmist saith of God, "Thine Arrows stick fast in me, and thy Hand presseth me sore." And yet nothing else, or more is meant by it, than when he saith, "My Sins have taken such Hold of me that I am not able to look up—My Iniquities are gone over my Head, and are like a sore Burden too heavy for me to bear."

[Love-2.2-50] Now, whether you call this State of Man the *Burden* of his Sins and Wickednesses, or the *Arrows* of the Almighty, and the *Weight* of God's Hand, they mean but one and the same Thing, which can only be called by these different Names, for no other Reason but this, because Man's *own* original Righteousness, which he had *from* God, makes his sinful State a Pain and Torment to him, and lies heavy upon him in every Commission of Sin. And when the Psalmist again saith, "Take thy Plague away from me, I am even consumed by means of thy heavy Hand," it is only praying to be delivered from his *own Plague*, and praying for the *same Thing* as when he saith, in other Words, "Make me a clean Heart, O God, and renew a right Spirit within me."

[Love-2.2-51] Now this Language of Scripture, which teaches us to call the Pains and Torments of our Sins, the *Arrows*, *Darts*, and *Strokes* of God's Hand upon us, which calls us to own the Power, Presence, and Operation of God, in all that we feel and find in our own inward State, is the Language of the most exalted Piety, and highly suitable to that Scripture which tells us, "That in God we live, and move, and have our Being". For by teaching us to find, and own the Power and Operation of God in every Thing that passes within us, it keeps us continually turned to God for all that we want, and by all that we feel within ourselves, and brings us to this best of all Confessions, that Pain, as well as Peace of Mind, is the Effect and Manifestation of God's infinite Love and Goodness toward us.

[Love-2.2-52] For we could not have this Pain and Sensibility of the Burden of Sin, but because the Love and Goodness of God made us *originally righteous* and *happy*; and therefore, all the Pains and Torments of Sin come from God's *first Goodness* toward us, and are in themselves merely and truly the Arrows of his Love, and his blessed Means of drawing us back to that first righteous State in and for which his first and never ceasing Love created us.

[Love-2.2-53] *Eusebius*. The Matter, therefore, plainly stands thus. There is no *righteous* Wrath, or *vindictive* Justice in the Deity itself, which, as a *Quality* or *Attribute* of Resentment in the Divine Mind, *wants* to be contented, atoned, or satisfied; but Man's Original *Righteousness,* which was once his *Peace*, and *Happiness*, and *Rest* in God, is by the Fall of *Adam* become his *Tormentor*, his *Plague*, that continually exercises its *good Vengeance* upon him, till it truly regains its first State in him.

[Love-2.2-54] *Secondly*, Man must be under this *Pain, Punishment*, and *Vengeance* to all Eternity; there is no Possibility, in the Nature of the Thing, for it to be otherwise, though God be all Love, unless Man's lost Righteousness be fully again possessed by him. And, therefore, the Doctrine of God's being all Love, of having no Wrath in Himself, has nothing in it to abate the

Force of those Scriptures which threaten Punishment to Sinners, or to make them less fearful of living and dying in their Sins.

[Love-2.2-55] *Theophilus.* What you say, *Eusebius*, is very true; but then it is but half the Truth of this Matter. You should have added, that this Doctrine is the one Ground, and only Reason, why the Scriptures abound with so many Declarations of *Woe, Misery*, and *Judgments,* sometimes executed, and sometimes only threatened by God, and why all Sinners to the End of the World must know and *feel* "that the Wrath of God is revealed from Heaven against all Ungodliness and Unrighteousness, and that Indignation and Wrath, Tribulation and Anguish, must be upon every Soul of Man that doth Evil" (Rom. 1:18, 2:8-9).

[Love-2.2-56] For all these Things, which the Apostle elsewhere calls "the Terrors of the Lord", have no *Ground*, nothing that *calls* for them, nothing that *vindicates* the Fitness and Justice of them, either with Regard to God or Man, but this one Truth, *viz.,* That God is in Himself a mere Infinity of Love, from whom nothing but outflowings of Love and Goodness can come forth from Eternity to Eternity. For if God is all Love, if he wills nothing toward fallen Man but his full Deliverance from the blind Slavery and Captivity of his earthly, bestial Nature, then every kind of *Punishment, Distress*, and *Affliction,* that can extinguish the Lusts of the Flesh, the Lust of the Eyes, and the Pride of this Life, may and *ought* to be expected from God, merely because he is all Love and good Will toward fallen Man.

[Love-2.2-57] To say, therefore, as some have said, If God is all Love toward fallen Man, how can he *threaten* or *chastise* Sinners? This is no better than saying, If God is all Goodness in Himself, and towards Man, how can He do that in and to Man, which is for his Good? As absurd as to say, If the able Physician is all Love, Goodness, and good Will toward his Patients, how can he blister, purge, or scarify them, how can he order one to be trepanned, and another to have a Limb cut off? Nay, so absurd is this Reasoning, that if it could be proved, that God had no Chastisement for Sinners, the very Want of this Chastisement would be the greatest of all Proofs, that God was not all Love and Goodness toward Man.

[Love-2.2-58] The meek, merciful, and compassionate Jesus, who had no Errand in this World but to bless and save Mankind, said, "If thy *right Eye* or thy *right Hand* offend thee, pluck out the one, cut off the other, and cast them from thee." And that He said all this from mere Love, he adds, It is *better for thee* to do this, than that thy whole Body should be cast into Hell". Therefore, if the Holy Jesus had been wanting in this Severity, he had been wanting in true Love toward Man.

[Love-2.2-59] And therefore, the pure, mere Love of God, is *that alone* from which Sinners are justly to expect from God, that no Sin will pass unpunished, but that his Love will visit them with every Calamity and Distress, that can help to break and purify the bestial Heart of Man, and awaken in him true Repentance and Conversion to God. It is Love alone in the holy Deity, that Will allow no Peace to the wicked, nor ever cease its Judgments, till every Sinner is forced to confess, That it is *good for him that he has been in Trouble*, and thankfully own, That not the Wrath, but the Love of God, has plucked out that *right Eye*, cut off that *right Hand,* which he ought to have done, but would not do, for himself and his own Salvation.

[Love-2.2-60] Again, this Doctrine that allows of no Wrath in the Divine Mind, but places it all in the Evil State of fallen Nature and Creature, has every Thing in it that can prove to Man the dreadful Nature of Sin, and the absolute Necessity of totally departing from it. It leaves no Room for Self-Delusion, but puts an End to every false Hope, or vain seeking for Relief in any Thing else, but the total Extinction of Sin. And this it effectually does, by showing, that Damnation is no foreign, separate, or imposed State, that is brought in upon us, or adjudged to us by the Will of God, but is the inborn, natural, essential State of our own disordered Nature, which is absolutely impossible, in the Nature of the Thing, to be any Thing else but our *own Hell,* both here and hereafter, unless all Sin be separated from us, and Righteousness be again made our natural State, by a Birth of itself in us. And all this, not because God will have it so, by an arbitrary Act of his sovereign Will, but because he cannot change his own Nature, or make any Thing to be happy and blessed, but only that which has its proper Righteousness, and is of one Will and Spirit with Himself.

[Love-2.2-61] If then every Creature that has lost, or is without the true Rectitude of its Nature, must as such, be of all Necessity, absolutely separated from God, and necessarily under the Pain and Misery of a Life that has lost all its own natural Good; if no *Omnipotence* or *Mercy,* or *Goodness* of God, can make it to be otherwise, or give any Relief to the Sinner, but by a total Extinction of Sin by a Birth of Righteousness in the Soul, then it fully appears, that according to this Doctrine, every Thing in God, and Nature, and Creature, calls the Sinner to an absolute Renunciation of all Sin, as the *one only possible* Means of Salvation, and leaves no Room for him to deceive himself with the Hopes that any Thing else will do instead of it. Vainly therefore is it said, That if God be all Love, the Sinner is let loose from the dreadful Apprehensions of living and dying in his Sins.

[Love-2.2-62] On the other Hand, deny this Doctrine, and say, with the current of scholastic Divines, That the Sinner must be doomed to eternal Pain and Death, unless a supposed Wrath, in the Mind of the Deity, be first atoned and satisfied; and that Christ's Death was that valuable Gift, or Offering made to God, by which alone he could be moved to lay aside, or extinguish his own Wrath toward fallen Man; say this, and then you open a wide Door for Licentiousness and Infidelity in some, and superstitious Fears in others.

[Love-2.2-63] For if the Evil, the Misery, and sad Effects of Sin, are placed in a Wrath in the Divine Mind, what can this beget in the Minds of the pious, but superstitious Fears about a supposed Wrath in God which they can never know when it is, or is not, atoned? Every Kind of Superstition has its Birth from this Belief, and cannot well be otherwise. And as to the Licentious, who want to stifle all Fears of gratifying all their Passions, this Doctrine has a natural Tendency to do this for them. For if they are taught, that the Hurt and Misery of Sin, is not its *own natural* State, not owing to its *own Wrath* and *Disorder,* but to a Wrath in the Deity, how easy is it for them to believe, either that God may not be so full of Wrath as is given out, or that he may overcome it himself, and not keep the Sinner eternally in a Misery that is not his own, but wholly brought upon him from without, by a Resentment in the Divine Mind.

[Love-2.2-64] Again, this Account which the *Schools* give of the Sacrifice of Christ, made to atone a Wrath in the Deity by the infinite Value of Christ's Death, is that alone which helps *Socinians, Deists,* and Infidels of all Kinds, to such Cavils and Objections to the Mystery of our

Redemption, as neither have, nor can be silenced by the most able Defenders of that scholastic Fiction. The Learning of a *Grotius* or *Stillingfleet,* when defending such an Account of the Atonement and Satisfaction, rather increases than lessens the Objections to this Mystery: But if you take this Matter as it truly is in itself, *viz.,* That God is in Himself all Love and Goodness, therefore can be nothing else but all Love and Goodness toward fallen Man, and that fallen Man is subject to no Pain or Misery, either present or to come, but what is the natural, unavoidable, essential Effect of his own evil and disordered Nature, impossible to be altered by himself, and that the infinite, never ceasing Love of God, has given Jesus Christ in *all his Process,* as the highest, and only possible Means, that Heaven and Earth can afford, to save Man from himself, from his own Evil, Misery, and Death, and restore to him his original Divine Life. When you look at this Matter in this true Light, then a God, all Love, and an Atonement for Sin by Christ, not made to pacify a Wrath in God, but to bring forth, fulfill, and restore Righteousness in the Creature that had lost it, has every Thing in it that can make the Providence of God adorable, and the State of Man comfortable.

[Love-2.2-65] Here all Superstition and superstitious Fears are at once totally cut off, and every Work of Piety is turned into a Work of Love. Here every false Hope of every Kind is taken from the *Licentious*; they have no Ground left to stand upon: Nothing to trust to, as a *Deliverance* from Misery, but the *one total* Abolition of Sin.

[Love-2.2-66] The *Socinian* and the *Infidel* are here also robbed of all their Philosophy against this Mystery; for as it is not founded upon, does not teach an *infinite Resentment,* that could only be satisfied by an *infinite Atonement,* as it stands not upon the Ground of Debtor and Creditor, all their Arguments which suppose it to be such, are quite beside the Matter and touch nothing of the Truth of this blessed Mystery. For it is the very Reverse of all this, it declares a God that is all Love; and the Atonement of Christ to be nothing else in itself, but the highest, most natural, and efficacious Means through all the Possibility of Things, that the infinite Love and Wisdom of God could use, to put an End to Sin, and Death, and Hell, and restore to Man his first Divine State or Life. I say, the most natural, efficacious Means through *all the Possibilities* of Nature; for there is nothing that is *supernatural,* however mysterious, in the whole System of our Redemption; every Part of it has its Ground in the Workings and Powers of Nature, and all our Redemption is only Nature set right, or made to be that which it ought to be.

[Love-2.2-67] There is nothing that is *supernatural,* but God alone; every Thing besides Him is from and subject to the State of Nature. It can never rise out of it, or have anything contrary to it. No Creature can have either Health or Sickness, Good or Evil, or any State either from God, or itself, but strictly according to the Capacities, Powers, and Workings of Nature.

[Love-2.2-68] The Mystery of our Redemption, though it comes from the supernatural God, has nothing in it but what is done, and to be done, within the Sphere, and according to the Powers of Nature. There is nothing supernatural in it, or belonging to it, but that supernatural Love and Wisdom which brought it forth, presides over it, and will direct it till Christ, as a second *Adam,* has removed and extinguished all that Evil, which the first *Adam* brought into the human Nature.

[Love-2.2-69] And the whole Process of Jesus Christ, from his being the inspoken *Word* or *Bruiser* of the Serpent given to *Adam,* to his Birth, Death, Resurrection, and Ascension into

Heaven, has all its Ground and Reason in this, because nothing else in all the Possibilities of Nature, either in Heaven or on Earth, could *begin, carry* on, and *totally* effect Man's Deliverance from the Evil of his own fallen Nature.

[Love-2.2-70] Thus is Christ the one, full, sufficient Atonement for the Sin of the whole World, because He is the one *only natural* Remedy, and *possible* Cure of all the Evil that is broken forth in Nature, the one *only natural Life,* and *Resurrection* of all that Holiness and Happiness that died in *Adam.* And seeing all this Process of Christ is given to the World, from the supernatural, antecedent, infinite Love of God, therefore it is, that the Apostle saith, "God was in Christ reconciling the World to Himself." And Christ in God, is nothing else in his whole Nature, but that same, *certain*, and *natural* Parent of a Redemption to the whole human Nature, as *fallen Adam* was the *certain* and *natural* Parent of a miserable Life to every Man that is descended from him: With this only Difference, that from fallen *Adam* we are born in Sin, whether we will or no, but we cannot have the new Birth which Christ has all Power to bring forth in us, unless the Will of our Heart closes with it.

[Love-2.2-71] But as nothing came to us from *Adam,* but according to the Powers of Nature, and because he was that which he was with Relation to us; so it is with Christ and our Redemption by Him: All the Work is grounded in, and proceeds according to the Powers of Nature, or in a Way of natural Efficacy or Fitness to produce its Effects; and every Thing that is found in the Person, Character, and Condition of Christ, is only there as his *true* and *natural* Qualification to do all that He came to do, in us, and for us. That is to say, Christ was made to be that which He was; He was a *Seed* of Life in our first fallen Father; He lived as a *Blessing of Promise* in the Patriarchs, Prophets, and Israel of God; He was born as a Man of a pure Virgin; He did all that He did, whether as suffering, dying, conquering, rising, and ascending into Heaven, only as so many Things, which as *naturally* and as *truly,* according to the Nature of Things, qualified Him to be the Producer, or Quickener of a Divine Life in us, as the State and Condition of *Adam* qualified him to make us the slavish Children of earthly, bestial Flesh and Blood.

[Love-2.2-72] This is the comfortable Doctrine of our Redemption; nothing in God but an Infinity of Love and Goodness toward our fallen Condition; nothing in Christ, but that which had its *Necessity* in the Nature of Things, to make Him able to give, and us to receive, our full Salvation from Him.

[Love-2.2-73] I will now only add, That from the Beginning of Deism, and from the Time of *Socinus,* to this Day, not a Socinian or Deist has ever seen or opposed this Mystery in its true State, as is undeniably plain from all their Writings.

[Love-2.2-74] A late Writer, who has as much Knowledge, and Zeal, and Wit in the Cause of Deism, as any of his Predecessors, is forced to attack our Redemption by giving this false Account of it.

[Love-2.2-75] "That a perfectly innocent Being, of the highest Order among intelligent Natures, should personate the Offender, and suffer in his Place and Stead, in order to take down the Wrath and Resentment of the Deity against the Criminal, and dispose God to show Mercy to him,—the

Deist conceives to be both unnatural, and improper, and therefore not to be ascribed to God without Blasphemy."

[Love-2.2-76] *And again,* "The common Notion of Redemption among Christians seems to represent the Deity in a disagreeable Light, as implacable and revengeful," *&c.*

[Love-2.2-77] What an Arrow is here, I will not say, shot beside the Mark, but shot at nothing! Because nothing of that, which he accuses is to be found in our Redemption. The God of Christians is so far from being, as he says, *implacable* and revengeful, that you have seen it proved from Text to Text, that the whole Form and Manner of our Redemption comes wholly from the free, antecedent, infinite Love and Goodness of God towards fallen Man. That the *innocent Christ* did not suffer, to quiet an angry Deity, but merely as *co-operating, assisting,* and *uniting* with that Love of God, which desired our Salvation. That He did not suffer in *our Place or Stead,* but only *on our Account,* which is a quite different Matter. And to say, that He suffered in *our Place or Stead,* is as absurd, as contrary to Scripture, as to say, that He rose from the Dead, and Ascended into Heaven in *our Place and Stead,* that we might be excused from it. For his Sufferings, Death, Resurrection, and Ascension are all of them equally on *our Account,* for our Sake, for our Good and Benefit, but none of them possible to be in our Stead.

[Love-2.2-78] And as Scripture and Truth affirm, that He ascended into Heaven *for us,* though neither Scripture nor Truth will allow it to be in *our Place and Stead,* so for the same Reasons, it is strictly true, that He suffered, and died *for us,* though no more in our *Place* or *Stead,* nor any more desirable to be so, than his Ascension into Heaven for us should be in *our Place and Stead.*

[Love-2.2-79] I have quoted the above Passage, only to show you, that a Defender of Deism, however acute and ingenious, has not one Objection to the Doctrine of our Redemption, but what is founded on the grossest Ignorance, and total Mistake of the whole Nature of it. But when I lay this gross Ignorance to the Deists' Charge, I do not mean any natural Dullness, Want of Parts, or Incapacity in them to judge aright, but only that something or other, either Men or Books, or their own Way of Life, has hindered their seeing the true Ground and real Nature of Christianity, as it is in itself.

[Love-2.2-80] *Eusebius.* I would fain Hope, *Theophilus,* that from all that has been said in the *Demonstration of the Fundamental Errors of the Plain Account,* the *Appeal to all that doubt, &c.,* and the rest that follow, to these Dialogues; in all which, Christianity and Deism, with their several Merits, are so plainly, and with so much good Will and Affection toward all Unbelievers, represented to them, all that are serious and well-minded amongst the Deists will be prevailed upon to reconsider the Matter. For though some People have been hasty enough to charge those Writings with Fanaticism, or Enthusiasm, as disclaiming the Use of our Reason in Religious Matters, yet this Charge can be made by none, but those who, having not read them, take up with hearsay Censures.

[Love-2.2-81] For in those Books, from the Beginning to the End, nothing is appealed to but the natural Light of the Mind, and the plain, known Nature of Things; no one is led, or desired to go one Step further. The *Use of Reason* is not only allowed, but asserted, and proved to be of the *same Service* to us in Things of Religion, as in Things that relate to our Senses in this World *{Demonstration of Errors of the Plain Account}*.

[Love-2.2-82] The true Ground, Nature, and Power of *Faith* is opened, by fully proving, that this Saying of Christ, "According to thy Faith, so be it done unto Thee," takes in every Individual of human Nature; and that all Men, whether *Christians, Deists, Idolaters,* or *Atheists,* are all of them equally Men of *Faith*, all equally, and absolutely governed by it, and therefore must have all that they have, Salvation or Damnation, strictly and solely according to their Faith *{Way to Divine Knowledge}*. All this is so evidently proved, that I can't help thinking, but that every considerate Reader must be forced to own it.

[Love-2.2-83] *Theogenes*. All this is well said. But let us now return to the finishing of our main Point, which was to show, that the Doctrine of *a God all Love,* does not only not destroy the Necessity of Christ's Death and the infinite Value and Merits of it, but is itself the fullest Proof and strongest Confirmation of both.

[Love-2.2-84] *Theophilus*. How it could enter into anyone's Head, to charge this Doctrine with destroying the *Necessity* and Merits of Christ's Death, is exceeding strange.

[Love-2.2-85] For look where you will, no other Cause, or Reason of the Death of Christ, can be found but in the Love of God toward fallen Man. Nor could the Love of God will or accept of the Death of Christ, but because of its absolute Necessity, and availing Efficacy to do all that for fallen Man, which the Love of God would have to be done for him.

[Love-2.2-86] God did not, could not, love or like or desire the Sufferings and Death of Christ, for what they were in themselves, or as Sufferings of the highest Kind. No, the higher and greater such Sufferings had been, were they only considered in themselves, the less pleasing they had been to a God, that wills nothing but Blessing and Happiness to every Thing capable of it.

[Love-2.2-87] But all that Christ *was* and *did* and *suffered* was infinitely prized, and highly acceptable to the Love of God, because all that Christ was, and did, and suffered in his own Person, was *That* which gave him full Power, to be a common Father of Life to all that died in *Adam*.

[Love-2.2-88] Had Christ wanted anything that he was, or did, or suffered in his own Person, he could not have stood in that Relation to all Mankind as *Adam* had done. Had he not been given to the first fallen Man, as *a Seed of the* Woman, as a *Light* of Life, *enlightening every Man that comes into the World*, He could not have had *his Seed* in every Man, as *Adam* had, nor been as universal a Father of Life, as *Adam* was of Death. Had he not in the Fitness, or Fullness of Time, become a Man, born of a pure Virgin, the first Seed of Life in every Man, must have lain only as a Seed, and could not have come to the Fullness of the Birth of a new Man in Christ Jesus. For the Children can have no other State of Life, but that which their Father first had. And therefore Christ, as the Father of a regenerated human Race, must first stand in the Fullness of that human State, which was to be derived from him into all his Children.

[Love-2.2-89] This is the absolute Necessity of Christ's being all that he was, *before* he became Man; a Necessity arising from the Nature of the Thing. Because he could not possibly have had the Relation of a Father to all Mankind, nor any Power to be a Quickener of a Life of Heaven in them, but because He was both God in himself, and a Seed of God in all of them.

[Love-2.2-90] Now all that Christ was, and did, and suffered, *after* He became Man, is from the same Necessity founded in the Nature of the Thing. He suffered on no other Account, but because that which he came to do in, and for the human Nature, was and could be nothing else in itself, but a Work of Sufferings and Death.

[Love-2.2-91] A crooked Line cannot become straight, but by having all its Crookedness given up, or taken from it. And there is but one Way possible in Nature for a crooked Line to lose its Crookedness.

[Love-2.2-92] Now the Sufferings and Death of Christ stand in this kind of Necessity. He was made Man for our Salvation, that is, He took upon Him our fallen Nature, to bring it out of its *evil crooked* State, and set it again in that Rectitude in which it was created.

[Love-2.2-93] Now there was no more two Ways of doing this, than there are two Ways of making a crooked Line to become straight.

[Love-2.2-94] If the Life of fallen Nature, which Christ had taken upon Him, was to be overcome by Him, then every Kind of suffering and dying, that was a giving up, or departing from the Life of fallen Nature, was just as necessary, in the Nature of the Thing, as that the Line to be made straight must give up, and Part with every Kind and Degree of its own Crookedness.

[Love-2.2-95] And therefore the Sufferings and Death of Christ were, in the Nature of the Thing, the only possible Way of his acting contrary to, and overcoming all the Evil that was in the fallen State of Man.

[Love-2.2-96] The Apostle saith, "The Captain of our Salvation was to be made perfect through Sufferings." This was the Ground and Reason of his Sufferings. Had he been without them, He could not have been perfect in Himself, as a *Son of Man,* nor the Restorer of Perfection in all Mankind. But why so? Because his Perfection, as a *Son of Man,* or the Captain of *human Salvation,* could only consist in his acting in, and with a Spirit suitable to the first created State of perfect Man; that is, He must in his Spirit be as much above all the *Good* and *Evil* of this fallen World, as the first Man was.

[Love-2.2-97] But now, He could not show that He was of this Spirit, that He was under no Power of fallen Nature, but lived in the Perfection of the first created Man; He could not do this, but by showing, that all the Good of the earthly Life was renounced by Him, and that all the Evil which the World, the Malice of Men and Devils, could bring upon Him, could not hinder his living wholly and solely to God, and doing his Will on Earth with the same Fullness, as Angels do it in Heaven.

[Love-2.2-98] But had there been any Evil in all fallen Nature, whether in Life, Death, or Hell, that had not attacked Him, with *all its Force*, He could not have been said to have overcome it. And therefore so sure as Christ, the Son of Man, was to overcome the World, Death, Hell, and Satan, so sure is it, that all the Evils which they could *possibly* bring upon Him, were to be *felt* and *suffered* by Him, as absolutely necessary in the Nature of the Thing, to declare his Perfection, and prove his Superiority over them. Surely, my Friend, it is now enough proved to you, how a God all Love toward fallen Man, must love, like, desire, and delight in all the Sufferings of Christ, which alone could enable Him, as a Son of Man, to undo, and reverse all that Evil, which the first Man had done to all his Posterity.

[Love-2.2-99] *Eusebius*. Oh, Sir, in what an adorable Light is this Mystery now placed. And yet in no other Light than that in which in the plain Letter of all Scripture sets it. No Wrath in God, no fictitious Atonement, no Folly of Debtor and Creditor, no suffering in Christ for Sufferings' sake, but a Christ suffering and dying, as his *same Victory* over Death and Hell, as when He rose from the Dead and ascended into Heaven.

[Love-2.2-100] *Theophilus*. Sure now, *Eusebius*, you plainly enough see wherein the infinite Merits, or the availing Efficacy, and glorious Power of the Sufferings and Death of Christ consist; since they were that, in and through which Christ himself came out of the State of fallen Nature, and got Power to give the same Victory to all his Brethren of the human Race.

[Love-2.2-101] Wonder not, therefore, that the Scriptures so frequently ascribe all our Salvation to the Sufferings and Death of Christ, that we are continually referred to them, as the Wounds and Stripes by which we are healed, as the Blood by which we are washed from our Sins, as the Price (much above Gold and precious Stones) by which we are bought.

[Love-2.2-102] Wonder not also that in the Old Testament, its *Service Sacrifices*, and *Ceremonies* were instituted to typify, and point at the great Sacrifice of Christ, and to keep up a continual Hope, strong Expectation, and Belief of it. And that in the New Testament, the Reality, the Benefits, and glorious Effects of Christ our Passover being actually sacrificed for us, are so joyfully repeated by every Apostle.

[Love-2.2-103] It is because Christ, as suffering and dying, was nothing else but Christ conquering and overcoming all the false Good, and the hellish Evil, of the fallen State of Man.

[Love-2.2-104] His Resurrection from the Grave, and Ascension into Heaven, though great in themselves, and necessary Parts of our Deliverance, were yet but the Consequences and genuine Effects of his Sufferings and Death. These were in themselves the Reality of his Conquest; all his great Work was done and effected in them and by them, and his Resurrection and Ascension were only his entering into the Possession of that, which his Sufferings and Death had gained for him.

[Love-2.2-105] Wonder not then, that all the true Followers of Christ, the Saints of every Age, have so gloried in the Cross of Christ, have imputed such great Things to it, have desired nothing so much, as to be Partakers of it, to live in constant Union with it. It is because his Sufferings, his Death, and Cross, were the *Fullness* of his Victory over all the Works of the Devil. Not an *Evil* in

Flesh and Blood, not a *Misery* of Life, not a Chain of Death, not a *Power* of Hell and Darkness, but were all baffled, broken, and overcome by the Process of a suffering, and dying Christ. Well therefore may the Cross of Christ be the Glory of Christians.

[Love-2.2-106] *Eusebius*. This Matter is so solidly and fully cleared up, that I am almost ashamed to ask you any Thing further about it. Yet explain a little more, if you please, how it is, that the Sufferings and Death of Christ, gave Him Power to become a *common Father* of Life to all that died in *Adam*. Or how it is, that we, by Virtue of them, have Victory over all the Evil of our fallen State.

[Love-2.2-107] *Theophilus*. You are to know, *Eusebius*, that the Christian Religion is no *arbitrary System* of Divine worship, but is the one true, real, and only Religion of Nature; that is, it is wholly founded in the Nature of Things, has nothing in it supernatural or contrary to the Powers and Demands of Nature; but all that it does, is only in, and by, and according to the Workings and Possibilities of Nature.

[Love-2.2-108] A Religion that is not founded in Nature, is all Fiction and Falsity, and as mere a nothing as an *Idol*. For as no Creature can be, or have any Thing, but what it is and has from the Nature of Things, nor have any Thing done to it, Good or Harm, but according to the unalterable Workings of Nature, so no Religion can be of any Service, but that which works with and according to the Demands of Nature. Nor can any fallen Creature be raised out of its fallen State, even by the Omnipotence of God, but according to the Nature of Things, or the unchangeable Powers of Nature; for Nature is the Opening and Manifestation of the Divine Omnipotence; it is God's *Power-world*; and therefore all that God doth, is and must be done in and by the Powers of Nature. God, though omnipotent, can give no Existence to any Creature, but it must have that Existence in *Space* and *Time*.— Time cometh out of the *Eternity*, and Space cometh out of the *Infinity* of God—God hath an omnipotent Power over them, in them, and with them, to make both of them set forth and manifest the Wonders of his supernatural Deity. Yet Time can only be subservient to the Omnipotence of God, according to the Nature of Time; and Space can only obey his Will, according to the Nature of Space; but neither of them can, by any Power, be made to be in a supernatural State, or be any Thing but what they are in their own Nature.

[Love-2.2-109] Now Right and Wrong, Good and Evil, True and False, Happiness and Misery, are as unchangeable in Nature, as Time, and Space. And every State and Quality that is creaturely, or that can belong to any Creature, has its own Nature, as unchangeably as Time and Space have theirs.

[Love-2.2-110] Nothing therefore can be done to any Creature *supernaturally*, or in a Way that is *without,* or *contrary* to the Powers of Nature; but every Thing or Creature that is to be helped, that is to have any Good done to it, or any Evil taken out of it, can only have it done so far, as the Powers of Nature are able and rightly directed to effect it.

[Love-2.2-111] And this is the true Ground of all Divine Revelation, or that Help which the supernatural Deity vouchsafes to the fallen State of Man. It is not to appoint an arbitrary System of religious Homage to God, but solely to point out, and provide for Man, blinded by his fallen State, that *one only* Religion, that, according to the Nature of Things, can possibly restore to him his lost Perfection. This is the Truth, the Goodness, and the Necessity of the Christian Religion; it is true, and good, and necessary, because it is as much the *one only natural* and *possible* Way of overcoming all the Evil of fallen Man, as Light is the one only natural, possible Thing that can expel Darkness.

[Love-2.2-112] And therefore it is, that all the Mysteries of the Gospel, however high, are yet true and necessary Parts of the *one Religion* of Nature; because they are no higher, nor otherwise, than the *natural State* of fallen Man absolutely stands in Need of. His Nature cannot be helped, or raised out of the Evils of its present State, by any Thing less than these Mysteries; and therefore, they are in the same Truth and Justness to be called his *natural Religion,* as that *Remedy* which alone has full Power to remove all the Evil of a Disease, may be justly called its *natural Remedy.*

[Love-2.2-113] For a Religion is not to be deemed natural, because it has nothing to do with *Revelation*; but then is it the *one true Religion of Nature,* when it has every Thing in it that our *natural* State stands in need of; every Thing that can help us out of our present Evil, and raise and exalt us to all the Happiness which our Nature is capable of having. Supposing, therefore, the Christian scheme of Redemption to be all that, and nothing else in itself, but that which the *Nature of Things* absolutely requires it to be, it must, for that very Reason, have its *Mysteries.*

[Love-2.2-114] For the fallen, corrupt, mortal State of Man, absolutely requires these two Things as its only Salvation. *First*, the Divine Life, or the Life of God, must be revived in the Soul of Man. *Secondly*, there must be a Resurrection of the Body in a better State after Death. Now nothing in the Power of Man, or in the Things of this World, can effect this Salvation. If, therefore, this is to be the Salvation of Man, then some Interposition of the Deity is absolutely necessary, in the Nature of the Thing, or Man can have no Religion that is *sufficiently natural;* that is to say, no Religion that is sufficient, or equal to the Wants of his Nature.

[Love-2.2-115] Now this necessary Interposition of the Deity, though doing nothing but in a *natural* Way, or according to the Nature of Things, must be mysterious to Man, because it is doing something *more* and *higher* than his Senses or Reason ever saw done, or possible to be done, either by himself, or any of the Powers of this World.

[Love-2.2-116] And this is the true Ground and Nature of the Mysteries of Christian Redemption. They are, in themselves, nothing else but what the Nature of Things requires them to be, as natural, efficacious Means of our Salvation, and all their Power is in a *natural Way*, or *true Fitness* of Cause for its Effect; but they are mysterious to Man, because brought into the Scheme of our Redemption by the *Interposition* of God, to work in a Way and manner above, and superior to all that is seen and done in the Things of the World.

[Love-2.2-117] The Mysteries, therefore, of the Gospel are so far from showing the Gospel not to be the one *true* Religion of Nature, that they are the greatest Proof of it, since they are that alone which can help Man to all that good which his *natural State* wants to have done to it.

[Love-2.2-118] For instance, if the Salvation of Man absolutely requires the *Revival* or *Restoration* of the Divine Life in the human Nature, then nothing can be the *one, sufficient, true* Religion of Nature, but that which has a natural Power to do this.

[Love-2.2-119] What a Grossness of Error is it, therefore, to blame that Doctrine which asserts the Incarnation of the Son of God, or the Necessity of the Word being made Flesh, when in the Nature of the Thing, nothing else but this very Mystery can be the *natural, efficacious* Cause of the Renewal of the Divine Life in the human Nature, or have any natural Efficacy to effect our Salvation?

[Love-2.2-120] Having now, *Eusebius*, established this Ground, that nothing is, or can be a Part of true, natural Religion, or have any real *Efficacy,* as a Means of Salvation, but only that which has its *Efficacy* in and from the Nature of Things, or in the *natural Fitness* of Cause to produce its Effect, you are brought into the clear View of this Truth, *viz.,* That the Religion of *Deism* is *false*, and *vain*, and *visionary*, and to be rejected by every Man as the mere *enthusiastic, fanatic* Product of pure Imagination; and all for this plain Reason, because it quite disregards the *Nature* of Things, stands wholly upon a *supernatural* Ground, and goes as much *above* and as directly *contrary* to the Powers of Nature, as that *Faith* that trusts in, and prays to a *wooden* God.

[Love-2.2-121] I say not this (as is too commonly done) in the Spirit of Accusation, or to raise an Odium. No, by no Means. I have the utmost Aversion to such a Procedure; I would no more bring a false Charge against the *Deist*, than I would bear false Witness against an *Apostle*. And I desire to have no other Temper, Spirit or Behaviour toward them, but such as the loving God with all my Heart, and loving them as I Love myself, requires of me. And in this Spirit of Love, I charge them with *visionary* Faith, and *enthusiastic* Religion; and only so far, as I have from Time to Time proved, that they trust to be saved by that, which according to the unchangeable Nature of Things can have no Power of Salvation in it.

[Love-2.2-122] For a Religion, not grounded in the Power and Nature of Things, is *unnatural*, supernatural, *superrational*, and is rightly called either *Enthusiasm, Vision, Fanaticism, Superstition*, or *Idolatry*, just as you please. For all these are but different Names for one and the same religious Delusion. And every Religion is this Delusion, but that one Religion which is required by, and has its Efficacy in and from the unchangeable Nature of Things.

[Love-2.2-123] And thus stands the Matter betwixt the Deists and myself. If I knew how to do them or the Subject more Justice, I would gladly do it; having no Desire, either for them or myself, but that we may all of us be delivered from every Thing that separates us from God, all equal Sharers of every Blessing that He has for human Nature, all united in that Spirit of Love and Goodness for which he created us, and all blessed with that Faith and Hope to which the God of Love has called us, as the one, only, possible, natural, and full Means of ever finding ourselves saved, and redeemed from all the Evils both of Time and Eternity.

[Love-2.2-124] And now, *Eusebius*, upon this Ground, *viz.,* (1) That there is but one true Religion, and that it is the Religion of Nature. (2) That a Religion has no Pretense to be considered as the Religion of Nature, because it rejects Divine Revelation, and has only human Reason for its Guide, but wholly and solely because it has every Good in it that the *natural State* of Man wants, and can receive from Religion. (3) That nothing can be any religious Good, or have any real Efficacy, as a Means of Salvation, but only that which has its Efficacy in and from the natural Power of Things, or the Fitness and Sufficiency of Cause to produce its Effect. (4) That the Religion of the Gospel, in all its Mysteries and Doctrines, is wholly grounded in the natural Powers of Things, and their Fitness to produce their Effects. Upon this Ground I come to answer your Question, *viz.,* How it is that the Sufferings and Death of Christ gave Him full Power to become a *common Father of Life* to all those that died in *Adam*? Or how it is that we, by Virtue of them, are delivered out of all the Evils of our fallen State?

[Love-2.2-125] The Sufferings and Death of Christ have no *supernatural* Effect that is above, or contrary to Nature; because the Thing itself is impossible. For a Thing is only therefore impossible, because the Nature of Things will not allow it.

[Love-2.2-126] The Fall of all Mankind in *Adam* is no *supernatural* Event or Effect, but the natural and necessary Consequence of our Relation to him. Could *Adam* at his Fall into this earthly Life have absolutely overcome every Power of the World, the Flesh, and the Devil, in the same Spirit as Christ did, he had been his own Redeemer, had risen out of his Fall, and ascended into Paradise, and been the Father of a paradisiacal Offspring, just as Christ, when He had overcome them all, rose from the Dead, and ascended into Heaven. But *Adam* did not do this, because it was as impossible, in the Nature of the Thing, as for a Beast to raise itself into an Angel. If therefore Man is to come out of his fallen State, there must be something found out that, according to the Nature of Things, hath Power to effect it. For it can no more be done *supernaturally* by any Thing else, than it could by *Adam*.

[Love-2.2-127] Now the Matter stood thus: The Seed of all Mankind was in the Loins of fallen *Adam*. This was unalterable in the Nature of the Thing, and therefore all *Mankind* must come forth in his fallen State.

[Love-2.2-128] Neither can they ever be in any State whatever, whether earthly or heavenly, but by having an earthly *Man*, or a heavenly *Man* for their Father. For *Mankind,* as such, must of all Necessity be born of, and have that Nature which it hath from a *Man*. And this is the true Ground, and absolute Necessity of the one Mediator, the *Man* Christ Jesus. For seeing *Mankind,* as such, must have that Birth and Nature which they have from *Man*; seeing they never could have had any Relation to Paradise, or any Possibility of partaking of it, but because they had a paradisiacal Man for their Father, nor could have had any Relation to this earthly World, or any Possibility of being born earthly, but because they had an earthly Man for their Father; and seeing all this must be unalterably so forever, it plainly follows, that there was an utter Impossibility for the Seed of *Adam* ever to come out of its fallen State, or ever have another or better Life, than they had from Adam, unless *such a Son of Man* could be brought into Existence, as had the *same Relation* to all Mankind as *Adam* had, was as much in them all as *Adam* was, and had as full Power according to the *Nature of Things,* to give a heavenly Life to all the Seed in *Adam's* loins, as *Adam* had to bring them forth in earthly Flesh and Blood.

[Love-2.2-129] And now, Sir, that Christ was this very *Son of Man,* standing in the *same Fullness* of Relation to all Mankind as *Adam* did, having *his Seed* as really in them all, as Adam had, and as truly and fully qualified, according to the Nature of Things, to be a *common* and *universal* Father of Life, as *Adam* was of Death to all the human Race, shall in a Word or two be made as plain and undeniable, as that two and two are four.

[Love-2.2-130] The Doctrine of our Redemption absolutely asserts, that the *Seed* of Christ was sown into the first fallen Father of Mankind, called *the Seed of the Woman*, the *Bruiser* of the Serpent, the *ingrafted* Word of Life, called again in the Gospel, *that Light which lighteth every Man that cometh into the World.* Therefore Christ was in all Men, in that *same* Fullness of Relation of a Father to all Mankind, as the first *Adam* was. *Secondly*, Christ was born of *Adam's* Flesh and Blood, took the human Nature upon him, and therefore stood as a human Creature in the *same Relation* to Mankind, as *Adam* did. Nothing therefore was further wanting in Christ, to make him as truly a *natural Father of Life* to all Mankind, as *Adam* was at first, but God's Appointment of him to that End.

[Love-2.2-131] For as *Adam* could not have been the natural Father of Mankind, but because God created and appointed him for that End, so Christ could not have been the natural Regenerator, or Redeemer of a heavenly Life that was lost in all Mankind, but because God had appointed and brought him into the World for that End. Now that God did this, that Christ came into the World by Divine Appointment, to be the Saviour, the Resurrection and Life of all Mankind, is a Truth as evident from Scripture, as that *Adam* was the first Man.

[Love-2.2-132] And thus it appears, in the utmost degree of Plainness and Certainty, that Christ in his *single Person* was, according to the Nature of Things, as fully qualified to be a *common Redeemer*, as *Adam* was, in his single Person, to be a common Father of all Mankind. He had *his Seed* in all Mankind, as *Adam* had. He had the human Nature, as Adam had. And He had the same Divine Appointment as *Adam* had. But Christ, however qualified to be our Redeemer, could not be actually such, till He had gone through, and done all that, by which our Redemption was to be effected.

[Love-2.2-133] *Adam*, however qualified, yet could not be the Father of a paradisiacal Offspring, till he had stood out his Trial, and fixed Himself victorious over every Thing that could make Trial of Him. In like manner, Christ, however qualified, could not be the Redeemer of all Mankind, till he had also stood out his Trial, had overcome *all That* by which *Adam* was overcome, and had fixed Himself triumphantly in that Paradise which *Adam* had lost.

[Love-2.2-134] Now as Adam's Trial was, Whether he would keep Himself in his paradisiacal State, *above* and *free* from all that was Good and Evil in this earthly World? So Christ's trial was, Whether, as a *Son* of Man, and loaded with the *Infirmities* of fallen *Adam*, sacrificed to all that which the Rage and Malice of the World, Hell, and Devils could possibly do to him; whether He in the midst of all these Evils, could live and die with his Spirit as contrary to them, as much above them, as unhurt by them, as *Adam* should have lived in Paradise?

[Love-2.2-135] And then it was, that every Thing which had overcome *Adam*, was overcome by Christ; and Christ's Victory did, in the Nature of the Thing, as certainly and fully open an Entrance for Him, and all his Seed into Paradise, as *Adam's* Fall cast him and all his Seed into the Prison and Captivity of this earthly, bestial World.

[Love-2.2-136] Nothing *supernatural* came to pass in either Case, but Paradise lost, and Paradise regained, according to the Nature of Things, or the real Efficacy of Cause to produce its Effects.

[Love-2.2-137] Thus is your Question fully answered; *viz.,* How and why the Sufferings and Death of Christ enabled him to be the Author of Life to all that died in *Adam*? Just as the Fall of *Adam* into this World, under the Power of Sin, Death, Hell, and the Devil, enabled him to be the common Father of Death, or was the natural, unavoidable Cause of our being born under the same Captivity; just so, that Life, and Sufferings, and Death of Christ, which declared his breaking out from them, and Superiority over them, must in the Nature of the Thing as much enable Him to be the common Author of Life, that is, must as certainly be the *full, natural, efficacious* Cause of our inheriting Life from Him. Because, by what Christ was in Himself, by what He was in us, by his whole *State, Character*, and the Divine *Appointment*, we all had that *natural Union* with Him, and Dependence upon Him, as our Head in the Way of Redemption, as we had with *Adam* as our Head in the Way of our natural Birth. So that as it must be said, that because *Adam* fell, we must of all Necessity be Heirs of his fallen State, so with the same Truth and from the same Necessity of the Thing, it must be said, that because Christ our Head is risen victorious out of our fallen State, we as his Members, and having his Seed within us, must be and are made Heirs of all his Glory. Because in all Respects we are as *strictly,* as *intimately* connected with, and related to Him as the *one Redeemer,* as we are to *Adam* as the *one Father* of all Mankind. So that Christ by his Sufferings and Death become in all of us our Wisdom, our Righteousness, our Justification and Redemption, is the same sober and solid Truth, as *Adam* by his Fall become in all of us our Foolishness, our Impurity, our Corruption, and Death.

[Love-2.2-138] And now, my Friends, look back upon all that has been said, and then tell me, Is it possible more to exalt or magnify the infinite Merits, and availing Efficacy of the *Sufferings* and *Death* of Christ, than is done by this doctrine? Or whether every Thing that is said of them in Scripture, is not here proved, from the very Nature of the Thing, to be absolutely true? And again, Whether it is not sufficiently proved to you, that the Sufferings and Death of Christ are not only consistent with the Doctrine of a God all Love, but are the fullest and most absolute Proof of it?

[Love-2.2-139] *Eusebius*. Indeed, *Theophilus*, you have so fully done for us all that we wanted to have done, that we are now ready to take Leave of you. As for my Part, I want to return Home to enjoy my Bible, and delight myself with reading it in this comfortable Light, in which you have set the whole Ground and Nature of our Redemption. I am now in full Possession of this glorious Truth, that God is *mere Love*, the most glorious Truth that can possess and edify the Heart of Man. It drives every Evil out of the Soul, and gives Life to every Spark of Goodness that can possibly be kindled in it. Everything in Religion is made amiable, by being a Service of Love to the God of Love.

[Love-2.2-140] No Sacrifices, Sufferings, and Death, have any Place in Religion, but to satisfy and fulfill that Love of God, which could not be satisfied without our Salvation. If the Son of God is not spared, if He is delivered up to the Rage and Malice of Men, Devils, and Hell, it is because, had we not had such a Captain of our Salvation made perfect through Sufferings, it never could have been sung, "Oh Death, where is thy Sting, Oh Grave, where is thy Victory!" It never could have been true, that "as by one Man Sin entered into the World, and Death by Sin, so by one Man came the Resurrection of the Dead." It never could have been said " that as in Adam all die, so in Christ shall all be made alive."

[Love-2.2-141] Therefore, dear *Theophilus*, adieu. God is Love, and He that hath learnt to live in the Spirit of Love, hath learnt to live and dwell in God. Love was the Beginner of all the Works of God, and from Eternity to Eternity nothing can come from God, but a Variety of Wonders, and Works of Love, over all Nature and Creature.

[Love-2.2-142] *Theophilus*. God prosper, *Eusebius*, this Spark of Heaven in your Soul. May it, like the *Seraphim's Coal taken from the Altar*, purify your Heart from all its Uncleanness. But before you leave me, I beg one more Conversation to be on the *practical Part* of the Spirit of Love, that so Doctrine and Practice, hearing and doing, may go Hand in Hand.

The Third Dialogue Between Theogenes, Eusebius, and Theophilus

[Love-2.3-1] *EUSEBIUS*. You have shown great Good-will toward us, *Theophilus*, in desiring another Meeting before we leave you. But yet I seem to myself to have no Need of that which you have proposed by this Day's Conversation. For this Doctrine of the Spirit of Love cannot have more Power over me, or be more deeply rooted in me; than it is already. It has so gained and got Possession of my whole Heart, that every Thing else must be under its Dominion. I can do nothing else but love; it is my whole Nature. I have no Taste for any Thing else. Can this Matter be carried higher in Practice?

[Love-2.3-2] *Theophilus*. No higher, *Eusebius*. And was this the true State of your Heart, you would bid fair to leave the World as *Elijah* did; or like *Enoch* to have it said of you, that you lived wholly to love, and *was not*. For was there nothing but this Divine Love alive in you, your fallen Flesh and Blood would be in Danger of being quite burnt up by it. What you have said of yourself, you have spoken in great Sincerity, but in a total Ignorance of yourself, and the true Nature of the Spirit of Divine Love. You are as yet only charmed with the Sight, or rather the Sound of it; its real Birth is as yet unfelt, and unfound in you. Your natural Complexion has a great deal of the animal Meekness and Softness of the *Lamb* and the *Dove*, your Blood and Spirit are of this Turn; and therefore a God all Love, and a Religion all Love, quite transport you; and you are so delighted with it, that you fancy you have nothing in you but this God and Religion of Love. But, my Friend, bear with me, if I tell you, that all this is only the *good Part* of the Spirit of this bestial World in you, and may be in any unregenerate Man, that is of your Complexion. It is so far from being a genuine Fruit of Divine Love, that if it be not well looked to, it may prove a real Hindrance of it, as it oftentimes does, by its appearing to be that which it is not.

[Love-2.3-3] You have quite forgot all that was said in the Letter to you on the Spirit of Love, that it is a *Birth* in the Soul, that can only come forth in its proper Time and Place, and from its proper Causes. Now nothing that is a Birth can be taken in, or brought into the Soul by any notional Conception, or delightful Apprehension of it. You may love it as much as you please, think it the most charming Thing in the World, fancy everything but Dross and Dung in Comparison of it, and yet have no more of its Birth in you, than the blind Man has of that Light, of which he has got a most charming Notion. His Blindness still continues the same; he is at the same Distance from the Light, because Light can only be had by a *Birth* of itself in seeing Eyes. It is thus with the Spirit of Love; it is nowhere, but where it rises up as a Birth.

[Love-2.3-4] *Eusebius*. But if I am got no further than this, what Good have I from giving in so heartily to all that you have said of this Doctrine? And to what End have you taken so much Pains to assert and establish it?

[Love-2.3-5] *Theophilus*. Your Error lies in this; you confound two Things, which are entirely distinct from each other. You make no Difference betwixt the *Doctrine* that only sets forth the Nature, Excellence, and Necessity of the Spirit of Love, and the *Spirit* of *Love* itself; which yet are two Things so different, that you may be quite full of the former, and at the same Time quite empty of the latter. I have said every Thing that I could, to show you the Truth, Excellence, and Necessity of the Spirit of Love. It is of infinite Importance to you to be well established in the Belief of this Doctrine. But all that I have said of it, is only to induce and encourage you to buy it, at its own Price and to give all that for it, which alone can purchase it. But if you think (as you plainly do) that you have got it, because you are so highly pleased with that which you have heard of it, you only embrace the Shadow, instead of the Substance, of that which you ought to have.

[Love-2.3-6] *Eusebius*. What is the Price that I must give for it?

[Love-2.3-7] *Theophilus*. You must give up all that you are, and all that you have from fallen *Adam*; for all that you are and have from him is that Life of Flesh and Blood, which cannot enter into the Kingdom of God.

[Love-2.3-8] *Adam*, after his Fall, had nothing that was good in him, nothing that could inherit an eternal Life in Heaven, but the *Bruiser of the Serpent*, or the Seed of the Son of God that was reserved, and treasured up in his Soul. Every Thing else in him was *devoted* to Death, that this *incorruptible Seed of the Word* might grow up into a new Name in Christ Jesus.

[Love-2.3-9] All the Doctrine of God's *Reprobation* and *Election* relates wholly and solely to these two Things, *viz., the earthly bestial* Nature from *Adam*, and the *incorruptible Seed* of the Word, or *Immanuel* in every Man.

[Love-2.3-10] Nothing is *elected*, is *foreseen, predestinated*, or called according to the Purpose of God, but this Seed of the new Man, because the one eternal, unchangeable *Purpose* of God towards Man is only this, namely, that Man should be a heavenly Image, or Son of God. And therefore nothing can be elected, or called *according to the Purpose* of God, but this Seed of a heavenly Birth, because nothing else is able to answer, and fulfill the *Purpose* of God. But every Thing else that is in Man, his whole earthly, bestial Nature, is from Sin and is *quite contrary* to God's Purpose in the Creation of Man.

[Love-2.3-11] On the other Hand, nothing is *reprobated, rejected,* or cast out by God, but the *earthly Nature* which came from the Fall of *Adam*. This is the only *Vessel of Wrath*, the Son of *Perdition*, that can have no Share in the Promises and Blessings of God.

[Love-2.3-12] Here you have the whole *unalterable* Ground of Divine *Election* and *Reprobation*; it relates not to any particular Number of People or Division of Mankind, but solely to the two Natures that are, both of them, without Exception, in every Individual of Mankind. All that is earthly, serpentine, and devilish in every Man, is *reprobated* and *doomed* to Destruction; and the heavenly Seed of the new Birth in every Man, is *That* which is *chosen, ordained*, and *called* to eternal Life.

[Love-2.3-13] Election therefore and Reprobation, as respecting Salvation, equally relate to every Man in the World; because every Man, as such, hath *That* in him which *only* is elected, and that in him which only is reprobated, namely, the earthly Nature, and the heavenly Seed of the Word of God.

[Love-2.3-14] Now all this is evident, from the very Nature of the Thing. As soon as you but suppose Man at his Fall to have a Power of Redemption, or Deliverance from the Evil of his fallen Nature, engrafted into him, you then have the *first unchangeable* Ground of Election and Reprobation; you are infallibly shown what it is that God elects and reprobates, and the absolute Impossibility of any Thing else being reprobated by God, but that *fallen, evil* Nature from which he is to be redeemed, or of any Thing else being elected by God, but that Seed of a new *Birth,* which is to bring forth his Redemption.

[Love-2.3-15] Here therefore you have a full Deliverance from all Perplexity upon this Matter, and may rest yourself upon this great, comfortable, and most certain Truth, that *no other* Election or Reprobation, with regard to *Salvation,* ever did, or can belong to any one individual Son of *Adam*, but that *very same* Election and Reprobation, which *both of them* happened to, and took Place in *Adam's* individual Person. For all that which was in *Adam,* both as *fallen* and *redeemed*, must of all Necessity be in every Son of *Adam*; and no Man can possibly stand in any other Relation to God than *Adam* did, and therefore cannot have either more or less, or any other Divine Election and Reprobation than *Adam* had. For from the Moment of Man's Redemption, which began at the Fall, when the *incorruptible Seed of the Word* was given into *Adam*, every Son of *Adam*, to the End of the World, must come into it, under one and the same Election and Reprobation with Regard to God. Because the whole earthly Nature, from which Man was to be redeemed, and the Seed of the Word, by which he was to be redeemed, were both of them in every Man, one as certainly as the other.

[Love-2.3-16] Now this being the inward, essential State of every Man born into the World, having in himself all that is elected and all that is reprobated by God, hence it is that in order to publish the Truth and Certainty of such Election and Reprobation, and the Truth and Certainty of that two-fold Nature in Man, on which it is grounded, hence it is that the Spirit of God in holy Scripture, represents this Matter to us by such outward Figures, as are yet in themselves not figurative, but real Proofs of it.

[Love-2.3-17] This is first of all done under the Figures of *Cain* and *Abel*, the two first Births from *Adam*, where the one is murdered by the other, hereby demonstrating to us, by this Contrariety and Difference of these two first Births, the inward real State of the Father of them, namely, that the same two-fold Nature was in him, that discovered itself in these two first Births from him.

[Love-2.3-18] The same Thing is, age after age set forth in Variety of Figures, more especially *Ishmael* and *Isaac*, in *Esau* and *Jacob*. And all this, only further to confirm and establish this great Truth, viz., That such Strife and Contrariety as appeared in the Sons of the same Father, were not only outward Representations, but full Proofs of that inward Strife and Contrariety, which not only existed in their Fathers, but universally in every human Creature. For *Cain* and *Abel* had not come from *Adam*, but because both their Natures were antecedently in him, and in the same State of Opposition and Contrariety to each other. And as *Cain* and *Abel* were no other than the genuine Effects of the two-fold State, which *Adam* as *fallen* and *redeemed*, was then in, so every Man, descended from *Adam*, is in himself infallibly all that which *Adam* was, and has as certainly his own *Cain* and *Abel* within himself as *Adam* had. And from the Beginning to the End of the human Race, all that which came to pass so remarkably in the Births of *Cain* and *Abel*, *Ishmael* and *Isaac*, *Esau* and *Jacob*, all that same, some Way or other, more or less, comes to pass in every Individual of Mankind. In one Man, his *own Abel* is murdered by his own *Cain*, and in another, his own *Jacob* overcomes his own *Esau* that was born with him.

[Love-2.3-19] And all the Good or the Evil that we bring forth in our Lives, is from nothing else, but from the Strife of these *two Natures* within us, and their Victory over one another. Which Strife, no Son of *Adam* could ever have known anything of, had not the free Grace and Mercy of God *chosen* and *called* all Mankind to a new Birth of Heaven within them, out of their corrupt and fallen Souls. No possible War, or Strife of Good against Evil, could be in fallen Man, but by his having from God a Seed of Life in him, *ordained* and *predestinated* to overcome his earthly Nature. For that which is put into him by God, as the Power of his Redemption, must be contrary to that from which he is to be redeemed.

[Love-2.3-20] And thus a War of Good against Evil, set up within us, by the free Grace and Mercy of God to us, is the greatest of all Demonstrations, that there is but one Election, and but one Reprobation, and that all that God rejects and reprobates, is nothing else but that *corrupt Nature* which every individual Man, *Abel* as well as *Cain*, has in himself from *Adam* as *fallen*; and that all that God *elects, predestinates, calls, justifies*, and *glorifies*, is nothing else but that heavenly Seed, which every individual Man, *Pharaoh* as well as *Moses*, has in himself from *Adam*, as *redeemed*.

[Love-2.3-21] And thus you have an unerring Key to all that is said in Scripture of the Election falling upon *Abel*, *Isaac*, and *Jacob*, &c., and of the Reprobation falling upon *Cain*, *Ishmael*, and *Esau;* not because God has Respect to Persons, or that all Men did not stand before him in the same Covenant of Redemption; but the Scriptures speak thus, that the true Nature of God's Election and Reprobation may thereby be made manifest to the World.

[Love-2.3-22] For the *earthly Nature*, which God only reprobates, having broke forth in Predominance in *Cain, Ishmael*, and *Esau*, they became proper Figures of that which God reprobates, and were used by God as such. And the heavenly Seed, which is alone elected to eternal Glory, having broken forth in Predominance in *Abel, Isaac, Jacob, &c.*, they became proper Figures of that which God elects, and were used by God as such.

[Love-2.3-23] Nothing is here to be understood personally, or according to the Flesh of these Persons on either Side; but all that is said of them is only as they are Figures of the earthly Nature, and heavenly Seed in every Man. For nothing is reprobated in *Cain*, but that very same which is reprobated in *Abel, viz.,* the *earthly Nature*; nor is anything elected in *Jacob* but that very same which is equally elected in *Esau, viz.,* the *heavenly Seed*.

[Love-2.3-24] And now, Gentlemen, you may easily apprehend, *how* and *why* a God, in whose holy Deity no Spark of Wrath or Partiality can possibly arise, but who is from Eternity to Eternity only flowing forth in Love, Goodness, and Blessing to every Thing capable of it, could yet say of the Children, before they were born, or had done either Good or Evil, 'Jacob have I loved, and Esau have I hated. It is because *Esau* signifies the earthly, bestial Nature, that came from Sin; and *Jacob* signifies the *incorruptible Seed of the Word* that is to overcome *Esau* and change his Mortal into Immortality.

[Love-2.3-25] But now I stop, for you may perhaps think that I have here made a Digression from our proposed Subject.

[Love-2.3-26] *Eusebius*. A Digression you may call it, if you please, *Theophilus*, but it is such a Digression, as has entirely prevented my ever having one more anxious Thought about God's Decrees of Election and Reprobation.

[Love-2.3-27] The Matter now stands in open Daylight, notwithstanding that Thickness of learned Darkness, under which it has been hidden, from the Time of St. *Austin* to this Day. And now, Sir, proceed as you please, to lay open all my Defects, in the Spirit of Love; for I am earnestly desirous of being set right in so important a Matter.

[Love-2.3-28] *Theogenes*. Let me first observe to *Theophilus,* that I am afraid the Matter is much worse with me, than it is with you. For though this Doctrine seems to have got all my Heart, as it is a Doctrine, yet I am continually thrown out of it in Practice, and find myself as daily under the Power of my old Tempers and Passions, as I was before I was so full of this Doctrine.

[Love-2.3-29] *Theophilus*. You are to know, my Friends, that every Kind of Virtue and Goodness may be brought into us by two different Ways. They may be taught us outwardly by Men, by Rules and Precepts; and they may be inwardly born in us, as the genuine Birth of our own renewed Spirit. In the former Way, as we learn them only from Men, by Rules and Documents of Instruction, they at best only change our outward Behaviour and leave our Heart in its natural State, and only put our Passions under a forced Restraint, which will occasionally break forth in spite of the dead Letter of Precept and Doctrine. Now this Way of Learning and attaining Goodness, though thus imperfect, is yet absolutely necessary, in the Nature of the Thing, and must first have its Time, and Place, and Work in us; yet it is only for a Time, as the *Law* was a Schoolmaster to the *Gospel*. We must first be Babes in Doctrine, as well as in Strength, before we can be Men. But of all this outward Instruction, whether from good Men, or the *Letter* of Scripture, it must be said, as the Apostle saith of the Law, "that it maketh nothing perfect;" and yet is highly necessary in order to Perfection.

[Love-2.3-30] The true Perfection and Profitableness of the holy written Word of God is fully set forth by St. *Paul* to *Timothy*: "From a Child," saith he, "thou hast known the Scriptures, which are able to make thee wise unto Salvation, which is by Faith in Christ Jesus." Now these Scriptures were the *Law and the Prophets,* for *Timothy* had known no other from his Youth. And as they, so all other Scriptures since, have no other Good or Benefit in them, but as they lead and direct us to a Salvation, that is not to be had in themselves, but from Faith in Christ Jesus. Their Teaching is only to teach us, where to seek and to find the Fountain and Source of all Light and Knowledge.

[Love-2.3-31] Of the Law, saith the Apostle, "it was a Schoolmaster to Christ:" Of the Prophets, he saith the same. "Ye have," says he, "a more sure Word of Prophecy, whereunto you do well, that ye take Heed, as unto a Light that shineth in a dark Place, until the Day dawn, and the Day-Star ariseth in your Hearts." The same Thing is to be affirmed of the Letter of the *New Testament*; it is but our Schoolmaster unto Christ, a Light like that of Prophecy, to which we are to take great Heed, until Christ, as the Dawning of the Day, or the Day-Star, ariseth in our Hearts. Nor can the Thing possibly be otherwise; no Instruction that comes under the Form of Words can do more for us, than Sounds and Words can do; they can only direct us to something that is better than themselves, that can be the true Light, Life, Spirit, and Power of Holiness in us.

[Love-2.3-32] *Eusebius*. I cannot deny what you say, and yet it seems to me to derogate from Scripture.

[Love-2.3-33] *Theophilus*. Would you then have me to say, that the *written Word* of God is that Word of God which liveth and abideth forever; that Word, which is the Wisdom and Power of God; that Word, which was with God, which was God, by whom all Things were made; that Word of God, which was made Flesh for the Redemption of the World; that Word of God, of which we must be born again; that Word which lighteth every Man, that cometh into the World; that Word, which in Christ Jesus is become Wisdom, and Righteousness, and Sanctification in us; would you have me say, that all this is to be understood of the *written Word* of God? But if this cannot possibly be, then all that I have said is granted, namely, that Jesus is alone *that Word* of God, that can be the Light, Life, and Salvation of fallen Man. Or how is it possible more to exalt the Letter of Scripture, than by owning it to be a true, outward, verbal Direction to the one only true Light, and Salvation of Man?

[Love-2.3-34] Suppose you had been a true Disciple of *John* the *Baptist,* whose only Office was to prepare the Way to Christ, how could you have more magnified his Office, or declared your Fidelity to him, than by going from his Teaching, to be taught by that Christ to whom he directed you? The *Baptist* was indeed a *burning and a shining Light*, and so are the holy Scriptures; "but he was not that Light, but was sent to bear Witness to that Light. That was the true Light, which lighteth every Man, that cometh into the World."

[Love-2.3-35] What a Folly would it be, to say that you had undervalued the Office and Character of *John the Baptist,* because he was not allowed to be the Light itself, but only a true Witness of it, and Guide to it? Now if you can show, that the written Word in the Bible can have any other, or higher Office, or Power, than such a *ministerial* one as the *Baptist* had, I am ready to hear you.

[Love-2.3-36] *Eusebius.* There is no Possibility of doing that.

[Love-2.3-37] *Theophilus.* But if that is not possible to be done, then you are come to the full Proof of this Point, *viz.,* that there are two Ways of attaining Knowledge, Goodness, Virtue, *&c.,* the one by the Ministry of outward, verbal Instruction, either by Men or Books, and the other by an inward Birth of Divine Light, Goodness, and Virtue, in our own renewed Spirit: and that the former is only in order to the latter, and of no Benefit to us, but as it carries us further than itself, to be united in Heart and Spirit with the Light, and Word, and Spirit of God. Just as the *Baptist* had been of no Benefit to his Disciples, unless he had been their Guide from himself to Christ.

[Love-2.3-38] But to come now closer to our Subject in Hand.

[Love-2.3-39] From this two-fold Light, or Teaching, there necessarily arises a two-fold State of Virtue and Goodness. For such as the Teacher, or Teaching is, such is the State and Manner of the Goodness, that can be had from it. Every Effect must be according to the Cause that produces it. If you learn Virtue and Goodness only from outward Means, from Men, or Books, you may be virtuous and good according to *Time,* and *Place,* and outward *Forms;* you may do Works of Humility, Works of Love and Benevolence, use Times and Forms of Prayer; all this Virtue and Goodness is suitable to this Kind of Teaching, and may very well be had from it. But the *Spirit* of Prayer, the *Spirit* of Love, and the Spirit of Humility, or of any other Virtue, are only to be attained by the Operation of the Light and Spirit of God, not outwardly teaching, but inwardly bringing forth a new-born Spirit within us.

[Love-2.3-40] And now let me tell you both, that it is much to be feared that you as yet stand only under this outward Teaching; your good Works are only done under Obedience to such Rules, Precepts, and Doctrines, as your Reason assents to, but are not the Fruits of a new-born Spirit within you. But till you are thus renewed in the Spirit of your Minds, your Virtues are only *taught Practices,* and grafted upon a corrupt Bottom. Every-thing you do will be a mixture of good and bad; your Humility will help you to Pride, your Charity to others will give Nourishment to your own Self-Love; and as your Prayers increase, so will the Opinion of your own Sanctity. Because, till the Heart is purified to the Bottom, and has felt the Axe at the Root of its Evil (which cannot be done by outward Instruction) every Thing that proceeds from it partakes of its Impurity and Corruption.

[Love-2.3-41] Now that *Theogenes* is only under the Law, or outward Instruction, is too plain from the Complaint that he made of himself. For notwithstanding his Progress in the Doctrine of Love, he finds all the Passions of his corrupt Nature still alive in him, and himself only altered in Doctrine and Opinion.

[Love-2.3-42] The same may well be suspected of you, *Eusebius*, who are so mistaken in the Spirit of Love, that you fancy yourself to be wholly possessed of it, from no other Ground, but because you embrace it, as it were, with open Arms, and think of nothing but living under the Power of it. Whereas, if the Spirit of Love was really born in you from its own Seed, you would account for its Birth, and Power in you, in quite another Manner than you have here done; you would have known the Price that you had paid for it, and how many Deaths you had suffered, before the Spirit of Love came to Life in you.

[Love-2.3-43] *Eusebius*. But surely, Sir, imperfect as our Virtues are, we may yet, I hope, be truly said to be in a State of Grace; and if so, we are under something more than mere outward Instruction. Besides, you very well know, that it is a Principle with both of us, to expect all our Goodness from the Spirit of God dwelling and working in us. We live in Faith and Hope of the Divine Operation; and therefore I must needs say, that your Censure upon us seems to be more severe than just.

[Love-2.3-44] *Theophilus*. Dear *Eusebius*, I censure neither of you, nor have I said one Word by Way of Accusation. So far from it, that I love and approve the State you are both in. It is good and happy for *Theogenes,* that he feels and confesses, that his natural Tempers are not yet subdued by Doctrine and Precept. It is good and happy for you also, that you are so highly delighted with the *Doctrine* of Love, for by this means each of you have your true Preparation for further Advancement. And though your State has this Difference, yet the same Error was common to both of you. You both of you thought, you had as much of the Spirit of Love as you could, or ought to have; and therefore *Theogenes* wondered he had no more Benefit from it; and you wondered that I should desire to lead you further into it. And therefore, to deliver you from this Error, I have desired this Conference upon the practical Ground of the Spirit of Love, that you may neither of you lose the Benefit of that good State in which you stand.

[Love-2.3-45] *Eusebius*. Pray therefore proceed as you please. For we have nothing so much at Heart, as to have the Truth and Purity of this Divine Love brought forth in us. For as it is the highest Perfection that I adore in God, so I can neither wish nor desire any Thing for myself, but to be totally governed by it. I could as willingly consent to lose all my Being, as to find the Power of Love lost in my Soul. Neither Doctrine, nor Mystery, nor Precept has any Delight for me, but as it calls forth the Birth, and Growth, and Exercise of that Spirit, which doth all that it doth, toward God and Man, under the one Law of Love. Whatever therefore you can say to me, either to increase the Power, manifest the Defects, or remove the Impediments of Divine Love in my Soul, will be heartily welcome to me.

[Love-2.3-46] *Theophilus*. I apprehend that you don't yet know what Divine Love is in itself, nor what is its *Nature* and Power in the Soul of Man. For Divine Love is *perfect Peace* and Joy, it is a *Freedom* from all Disquiet, it is all *Content* and mere *Happiness;* and makes every Thing to rejoice in itself. Love is the Christ of God; wherever it comes, it comes as the Blessing and Happiness of every natural Life, as the Restorer of every lost Perfection, a Redeemer from all Evil, a Fulfiller of all Righteousness, and a Peace of God which passeth all Understanding. Through all the Universe of Things, nothing is *uneasy, unsatisfied*, or *restless*, but because it is not governed by Love, or because its Nature has not reached or attained the *full Birth* of the Spirit of Love. For when that is done, every Hunger is satisfied, and all complaining, murmuring, accusing, resenting, revenging, and striving are as totally suppressed and overcome as the Coldness, Thickness, and Horror of Darkness are suppressed and overcome by the breaking forth of the Light. If you ask, why the Spirit of Love cannot be *displeased*, cannot be *disappointed*, cannot *complain, accuse, resent, or murmur*? It is because Divine Love desires nothing but itself; it is its own Good, it has all when it has itself, because nothing is good but itself, and its own working; for Love is God, and he that dwelleth in God, dwelleth in Love. Tell me now, *Eusebius*, are you thus blessed in the Spirit of Love?

[Love-2.3-47] Eusebius. Would you have me tell you that I am an Angel, and without the Infirmities of human Flesh and Blood?

[Love-2.3-48] *Theophilus*. No, but I would have you judge of your State of Love by these Angelic Tempers, and not by any Fervour or Heat that you find in yourself. For just so much, and so far as you are freed from the *Folly* of all earthly Affections, from all Disquiet, Trouble, and Complaint about this, or that, just so much, and so far is the Spirit of Love come to Life in you. For Divine Love is a new Life, and new Nature, and introduces you into a new World; it puts an End to all your former Opinions, Notions, and Tempers; it opens new Senses in you, and makes you see high to be low, and low to be high; Wisdom to be Foolishness, and Foolishness Wisdom; it makes Prosperity and Adversity, Praise and Dispraise, to be equally nothing. "When I was a Child," saith the Apostle, "I thought as a Child, I spake as a Child, but when I became a Man, I put away childish Things." Whilst Man is under the Power of Nature, governed only by worldly Wisdom, his Life (however old he may be) is quite childish; every Thing about him only awakens childish Thoughts, and Pursuits in him; all that he sees and hears, all that he desires or fears, likes or dislikes, that which he gets, and that which he loses, that which he hath, and that which he hath not, serve only to carry him from this Fiction of Evil to that Fiction of Good, from one Vanity of Peace to another Vanity of Trouble. But when Divine Love is born in the Soul, all childish Images of Good and Evil are done away, and all the *Sensibility* of them is lost, as the Stars lose their *Visibility* when the Sun is risen.

[Love-2.3-49] *Theogenes*. That this is the true Power of the Spirit of Divine Love, I am fully convinced from my own Uneasiness at finding, that my natural Tempers are not overcome by it. For whence could I have this Trouble, but because that little Dawning that I have of the Spirit of Love in me, maketh just Demands to be the one Light, Breath, and Power of my Life, and to have all that is within me overcome and governed by it. And therefore I find, I must either silence this small Voice of new-risen Love within me, or have no Rest from Complaints and Self-condemnation, till my whole Nature is brought into Subjection to it.

[Love-2.3-50] *Theophilus*. Most rightly judged, *Theogenes*. And now we are fairly brought to the one great *practical Point*, on which all our Proficiency in the Spirit of Love entirely depends, namely, *that all that we are, and all that we have from Adam, as fallen*, must be given up, absolutely denied and resisted, if the Birth of Divine Love is to be brought forth in us. For all that we are by *Nature* is in full Contrariety to this Divine Love, nor can it be otherwise; a Death to itself is its only Cure, and nothing else can make it subservient to Good; just as Darkness cannot be altered, or made better in itself, or transmuted into Light; it can only be subservient to the Light, by being *lost* in it and *swallowed* up by it.

[Love-2.3-51] Now this was the first State of Man; all the natural Properties of his creaturely Life, were hid in God, united in God, and glorified by the Life of God manifested in them, just as the Nature and Qualities of Darkness are lost and hid, when enlightened and glorified by the Light. But when Man fell from, or died to the Divine Life, all the natural Properties of his creaturely Life, having lost their Union in and with God, broke forth in their own natural Division, Contrariety, and War against one another, just as the Darkness, when it has lost the Light, must show forth its own Coldness, Horror, and other uncomfortable Qualities. And as Darkness, though in the *utmost Contrariety* to Light, is yet absolutely necessary to it, and without which no *Manifestation* or *Visibility* of Light could possibly be, so it is with the natural Properties of the creaturely Life; they are in themselves all Contrariety to the Divine Life, and yet the Divine Life cannot be communicated but in them and by them.

[Love-2.3-52] *Eusebius*. I never read, or heard of the Darkness being necessary to Light: It has been generally considered as a *negative* Thing, that was nothing in itself, and only signified an *Absence* of Light. But your Doctrine not only supposes Darkness to be something *positive*, that has a Strength and Substantiality in itself, but also to be *antecedent* to the Light, because *necessary* to bring it into Manifestation. I am almost afraid to hear more of this Doctrine. It Sounds harsh to my Ears.

[Love-2.3-53] *Theophilus*. Don't be frightened, *Eusebius*. I will lead you into no Doctrine, but what is strictly conformable to the Letter of Scripture, and the most orthodox Piety. The Scripture saith, "God is Light, and in Him is no Darkness at all"; therefore the Scripture affirmeth Light to be *superior*, absolutely *separate* from, and eternally *antecedent* to Darkness; and so do I. In this Scripture you have a noble and true Account of Light, what it is, where it is, and was, and always must be. It can never change its State or Place, be altered in itself, be anywhere, or in another Manner, than as it was, and will be, from and to all Eternity. When God said, "Let there be Light, and there was Light," no Change happened to eternal Light itself, nor did any Light then begin to be; but the Darkness of this World then only *began* to receive a Power, or Operation of the eternal Light upon it, which it had not before; or Eternity then began to open *some Resemblance* of its own Glory in the dark Elements, and Shadows of Time, and thus it is, that I assert the *Priority* and *Glory* of Light, and put all Darkness under its Feet, as impossible to be any Thing else but its Footstool.

[Love-2.3-54] *Eusebius*. I am quite delighted with this. But tell me now, how it is that Light can only be manifested in, and by Darkness.

[Love-2.3-55] *Theophilus*. The Scripture saith that "God dwelleth in the Light, to which no Man can approach": Therefore the Scripture teacheth, that Light in itself is, and must be *invisible* to Man, that it cannot be approached, or made manifest to him, but in and by *something* that is not Light. And this is all that I said, and the very same Thing that I said, when I affirmed that Light cannot be manifested, or have any *Visibility* to created Eyes, but in and through and by Darkness.

[Love-2.3-56] Light, as it is in itself, is only in the *Supernatural* Deity; and that is the Reason, why no Man or any created Being, can approach to it, or have any Sensibility of it, as it is in itself. And yet no Light can come into this World, but that in which God dwelt before any World was created. No Light can be in Time, but that which was the Light of Eternity. If therefore the

Supernatural Light is to manifest *something* of its incomprehensible Glory, and make itself, in *some Degree,* sensible and visible to the Creature, this supernatural Light must enter into *Nature*, it must put on *Materiality*. Now Darkness is the one only *Materiality* of Light, in and through which it can become the Object of creaturely Eyes; and till there is Darkness, there is no possible Medium, or Power, through which the *Supernatural* Light can manifest *something* of itself, or have *any* of its Glory visible to created Eyes. And the Reason why Darkness can only be the *Materiality* of Light, is this, it is because Darkness is the *one only Ground* of all Nature, and of all Materiality, whether in Heaven or on Earth. And therefore every Thing that is creaturely in Nature, that has any Form, Figure, or Substance, from the highest Angel in Heaven to the lowest Thing upon Earth, hath all that it hath of Figure, Form, or Substantiality only and solely from Darkness. Look at the glittering Glory of the *Diamond* and then you see the *one Medium,* through which the Glory of the incomprehensible Light can make *some* Discovery or Manifestation of itself. It matters not, whether you consider Heaven or Earth, eternal or temporal Nature, nothing in either State can be capable of visible Glory, Brightness, or Illumination, but that which standeth in the State of the Diamond, and has its *own Thickness* of Darkness. And if the Universe of eternal and temporal Nature is everywhere Light, it is because it has Darkness everywhere for its Dwelling Place. Light, you know, is by variety of modern Experiments declared to be *material*; the Experiments are not to be disputed. And yet all these Experiments are only so many Proofs, not of the *Materiality* of Light, but of our Doctrine, *viz.,* that *Materiality* is always along with *visible* Light, and also that Light can only open, and display something of itself, in and by Darkness, as its Body of Manifestation and Visibility. But Light cannot possibly be material, because *all Materiality,* as such, be it what and where it will, is nothing else but so much Darkness. And therefore to suppose Light to be material, is the same Absurdity, as to suppose it to be Darkness; for so much Materiality is so much Darkness, and it is impossible to be otherwise. Again, All *Matter* has but one Nature; it admits of neither more nor less, but wherever it is, all that is material is equally there. If therefore Light was material, all the Materiality in the World must be Light, and equally so. For no Materiality could be Light, unless Light was essential to Matter, as such, no more than any Materiality could be extended, unless Extension was essential to Matter as such.

[Love-2.3-57] *Eusebius*. What is it then, that you understand by the Materiality of Light?

[Love-2.3-58] *Theophilus*. No more than I understand by the Materiality of the *Wisdom, Mercy,* and *Goodness* of God, when they are made intelligible and credible to me, by the Materiality of *Paper* and *Ink, &c.* For Light is as *distinct* from, and *superior* to all *that Materiality*, in and by which it gives forth some Visibility of itself, as the Wisdom, Mercy, and Goodness of God, are distinct from and superior to all that *written Materiality,* in and through which they are made in some Degree intelligible, and credible to human Minds.

[Love-2.3-59] The incomprehensible Deity can make no *outward Revelation* of his Will, Wisdom, and Goodness, but by *articulate Sounds, Voices,* or *Letters* written on Tables of Stone, or such-like Materiality. Just so, the invisible, inaccessible, supernatural Light can make no *outward Visibility* of itself, but through such Darkness of Materiality, as is capable of receiving its Illumination. But as the Divine Will, Wisdom, and Goodness, when making outward Revelation of themselves, by the Materiality of Things, are not therefore material, so neither is the Light material when it outwardly reveals something of its invisible, incomprehensible Splendour and Glory, by and through the Materiality of Darkness.

[Love-2.3-60] All Light then, that is *natural*, and *visible* to the Creature, whether in Heaven, or on Earth, is nothing else but so much Darkness *illuminated*; and that which is called the Materiality of Light, is only the Materiality of Darkness, in which the Light incorporateth itself.

[Love-2.3-61] For Light can be only that *same invisible*, unapproachable Thing, which it always was in God, from all Eternity. And that which is called the Difference of Light, is only the Difference of that *Darkness,* through which the Light gives forth *different Manifestations* of itself. It is the same, whether it illuminates the Air, Water, a Diamond, or any other Materiality of Darkness. It has no more Materiality in itself, when it enlightens the Earth, than when it enlightens the Mind of an Angel, when it gives *Colour* to Bodies, than when it gives *Understanding* to Spirits.

[Love-2.3-62] Sight and Visibility is but *one Power* of Light, but Light is *all Power*; it is *Life* and every joyful *Sensibility* of Life is from it. "In Him," says the Apostle, "was Light, and the Light was the Life of Men." Light is all Things, and Nothing. It is *Nothing,* because it is *supernatural*; it is all Things, because every good Power and Perfection of every Thing is from it. No Joy, or Rejoicing in any Creature, but from the Power and Joy of Light. No Meekness, Benevolence, or Goodness, in Angel, Man, or any Creature, but where Light is the Lord of its Life. Life itself begins no sooner, rises no higher, has no other Glory than as the Light begins it and leads it on. Sounds have no Softness, Flowers and Gums have no Sweetness, Plants and Fruits have no Growth, but as the Mystery of Light opens itself in them.

[Love-2.3-63] Whatever is delightful and ravishing, sublime and glorious, in *Spirits, Minds* or *Bodies*, either in Heaven, or on Earth, is from the Power of the *supernatural* Light, opening its endless Wonders in them. *Hell* has no Misery, Horror, or Distraction, but because it has *no Communication* with the supernatural Light. And did not the supernatural Light stream forth its Blessings into this World, through the *Materiality* of the Sun, all outward Nature would be full of the Horror of Hell.

[Love-2.3-64] And hence are all the Mysteries and Wonders of Light, in this material *System,* so astonishingly great and unsearchable; it is because the *natural Light* of this World is nothing else but the Power and Mystery of the *supernatural Light,* breaking forth, and opening itself, according to its Omnipotence, in all the various Forms of elementary Darkness which constitute this temporary World.

[Love-2.3-65] *Theogenes*. I could willingly hear you, *Theophilus*, on this Subject till Midnight, though it seems to lead us away from our proposed Subject.

[Love-2.3-66] *Theophilus*. Not so far out of the Way, *Theogenes*, as you may imagine; for Darkness and Light are the *two Natures* that are in every Man, and do all that is done in him.

[Love-2.3-67] The Scriptures, you know, make only this Division: The Works of Darkness are Sin, and they who walk in the Light are the Children of God. Therefore Light and Darkness do every Thing, whether good or evil, that is done in Man.

[Love-2.3-68] *Theogenes.* What is this Darkness in itself, or where is it?

[Love-2.3-69] *Theophilus.* It is everywhere, where there is *Nature* and *Creature*. For all Nature, and all that is *natural* in the Creature, is in itself nothing else but Darkness, whether it be in Soul or Body, in Heaven or on Earth. And therefore, when the Angels (though in Heaven) had lost the *supernatural Light*, they became imprisoned in the Chains of their *own natural* Darkness. If you ask, Why Nature must be Darkness? It is because Nature is not God, and therefore can have no Light as it is Nature. For God and *Light* are as *inseparable,* as God and *Unity* are inseparable. Every Thing, therefore, that is not God, is and can be nothing else in itself but *Darkness*, and can do nothing but in, and under, and according to the *Nature* and *Powers* of Darkness.

[Love-2.3-70] *Theogenes.* What are the Powers of Darkness?

[Love-2.3-71] *Theophilus.* The Powers of Darkness are the Workings of Nature or Self: For *Nature, Darkness*, and *Self* are but three different Expressions for one and the same Thing.

[Love-2.3-72] Now every evil, wicked, wrathful, impure, unjust Thought, Temper, Passion, or Imagination, that ever stirred or moved in any Creature; every Misery, Discontent, Distress, Rage, Horror, and Torment, that ever plagued the Life of fallen Man or Angel are the *very Things* that you are to understand by the *Powers* or Workings of Darkness, Nature, or Self. For nothing is evil, wicked, or tormenting, but that which Nature or Self doth.

[Love-2.3-73] *Theogenes.* But if Nature is thus the *Seat* and *Source* of all Evil, if every Thing that is bad is in it and from it, how can such a Nature be brought forth by God who is all Goodness?

[Love-2.3-74] *Theophilus.* Nature has *all* Evil, and *no* Evil in itself. Nature, as it comes forth from God, is Darkness without any Evil of Darkness in it; for it is not Darkness without, or *separate* from Light, nor could it ever have been known to have any Quality of Darkness in it, had it not lost that State of Light in which it came forth from God, only as a Manifestation of the Goodness, Virtues, and Glories of Light. *Again*, it is Nature, viz., a *Strife* and *Contrariety* of Properties for this only End, that the *supernatural Good* might thereby come into *Sensibility*, be known, found and felt, by its taking *all the Evil* of Strife and Contrariety from them, and becoming the *Union, Peace*, and *Joy* of them all. Nor could the *Evil* of Strife, and Contrariety of Will, ever have had a Name in all the Universe of Nature and Creature, had it all continued in *that State* in which it came forth from God. Lastly, it is *Self,* viz., an *own Life*, that so, through such an *own Life*, the universal, incomprehensible Goodness, Happiness, and Perfections of the Deity, might be possessed as Properties and Qualities of *an own Life* in creaturely finite Beings.

[Love-2.3-75] And thus, all that is called *Nature, Darkness*, or *Self,* has not only *no Evil* in it, but is the only true Ground of all possible Good.

[Love-2.3-76] But when the intelligent Creature turns from God to *Self* or Nature, he acts *unnaturally*, he turns from all that which makes Nature to be *good*, he finds Nature only as it is in *itself*, and *without* God. And then it is, that Nature, or Self, hath all Evil in it. Nothing is to be had from it, or found in it, but the Work and Working of every Kind of Evil, Baseness, Misery, and Torment, and the utmost Contrariety to God and all Goodness. And thus also you see the Plainness and Certainty of our Assertion, that Nature or Self hath all Evil, and no Evil in it.

[Love-2.3-77] *Theogenes*. I plainly enough perceive, that *Nature* or *Self*, without God manifested in it, is all Evil and Misery. But I would, if I could, more perfectly understand the precise Nature of *Self*, or what it is that makes it to be so full of Evil and Misery.

[Love-2.3-78] *Theophilus*. Covetousness, Envy, Pride, and Wrath, are the four Elements of *Self*, or *Nature*, or *Hell*, all of them inseparable from it. And the Reason why it must be thus, and cannot be otherwise, is because the *natural Life* of the Creature is brought forth for the Participation of some *high supernatural* Good in the Creator. But it could have no *Fitness* or possible *Capacity* to receive such Good, unless it was in itself both an Extremity of *Want*, and an extremity of *Desire* of some high Good. When, therefore, this *natural Life* is deprived of, or fallen from God, it can be nothing else in itself but an Extremity of *Want*, continually *desiring*, and an Extremity of *Desire*, continually wanting. And hence it is, that its whole Life can be nothing else but a Plague and Torment of Covetousness, Envy, Pride, and Wrath, all which is precisely *Nature, Self, or Hell*.

[Love-2.3-79] Now Covetousness, Pride, and Envy, are not three different Things, but only three different Names, for the restless Workings of *one* and the *same Will* or Desire, which, as it differently torments itself, takes different Names; for nothing is in any of them, but the working of a *restless Desire*, and all this because the natural Life of the Creature can do nothing else but work as a Desire. And therefore, when *fallen* from God, its *three first* Births, and which are quite inseparable from it, are Covetousness, Envy, and Pride. It must *covet*, because it is a Desire proceeding from *Want*; it must *envy*, because it is a Desire turned to *Self*; it must *assume* and *arrogate*, because it is a Desire founded on a real Want of *Exaltation*, or a higher State.

[Love-2.3-80] Now *Wrath*, which is a *fourth Birth* from these three, can have no Existence, till some or all of these three are *contradicted*, or have something done to them that is *contrary* to their Will; and then it is that *Wrath* is necessarily born, and not till then.

[Love-2.3-81] And thus you see in the highest Degree of Certainty, what *Nature* or *Self* is, as to its essential, constituent Parts. It is the *three* forementioned, *inseparable Properties* of a Desire thrown into a *fourth* of Wrath, that can never cease, because their Will can never be gratified. For these four Properties generate one another, and therefore generate their own Torment. They have no outward Cause, nor any inward Power of altering themselves. And therefore, all *Self*, or *Nature*, must be in this State till some *supernatural Good* comes into it, or gets a Birth in it. And therefore, every Pain or Disorder, in the Mind or Body of any intelligent Creature, is an undeniable Proof that it is in a fallen State, and has lost that *supernatural Good* for which it was created. So certain a Truth is the fallen State of all Mankind. And here lies the absolute, indispensable Necessity of the one Christian Redemption. Till fallen Man is born again from above, till such a *supernatural Birth* is brought forth in him, by the eternal *Word* and *Spirit* of God, he can have no possible Escape or Deliverance from these four Elements of *Self* or *Hell*.

[Love-2.3-82] Whilst Man indeed lives amongst the Vanities of Time, his Covetousness, Envy, Pride, and Wrath, may be in a tolerable State, may help him to a Mixture of Peace and Trouble; they may have at Times their Gratifications, as well as their Torments. But when Death has put an End to the Vanity of all earthly Cheats, the Soul that is not born again of the *supernatural Word* and *Spirit* of God, must find itself unavoidably devoured, or shut up in its own, insatiable, unchangeable, self-tormenting Covetousness, Envy, Pride, and Wrath. Oh! *Theogenes*, that I had Power from God to take those dreadful Scales from the Eyes of every Deist, which hinder him from seeing and feeling the infinite importance of this most certain Truth!

[Love-2.3-83] *Theogenes*. God give a Blessing, *Theophilus*, to your good Prayer. And then let me tell you, that you have quite satisfied my Question about the Nature of *Self*. I shall never forget it, nor can I ever possibly have any Doubt of the Truth of it.

[Love-2.3-84] *Theophilus*. Let me however go a little deeper in the Matter. All Life, and all Sensibility of Life, is a *Desire*; and nothing can feel or find itself to exist, but as it finds itself to *have* and *be* a Desire; and therefore, all Nature is a *Desire*; and all that Nature does, or works, is done by the *Working* of Desire. And this is the Reason why all Nature, and the natural Life of every Creature, is a State of *Want*, and therefore must be a State of Misery and Self-Torment, so long as it is *mere Nature,* or left to itself. For every Desire, as *such*, is and must be made up of *Contrariety*, as is sufficiently shown elsewhere. *{ Way to Divine Knowledge; Spirit of Love. }* And its essential Contrariety, which it has in itself, is the one *only possible* Beginning or Ground of its Sensibility. For nothing can be felt, but because of Contrariety to *that* which feels. And therefore no creaturely Desire can be brought into Existence, or have any possible Sensibility of itself, but because *Desire,* as such, is unavoidably made up of *that Contrariety,* whence comes all *Feeling,* and the Capacity of being *felt*.

[Love-2.3-85] *Again*, All natural Life is nothing else but a mere Desire founded in *Want*; now *Want* is contrary to *Desire*; and, therefore every natural Life, *as such*, is in a State of *Contrariety* and *Torment* to itself. It can do nothing but work in, and feel its own Contrariety, and so be its own unavoidable, incessant Tormentor.

[Love-2.3-86] Hence we may plainly see, that God's bringing a sensible Creature into Existence is his bringing the *Power* of *Desire* into a *creaturely State*; and the Power and Extent of its own working Desire is the *Bounds* or *Limits* of its own creaturely Nature. And, therefore every intelligent Creature, of whatever Rank in the Creation, is and can be nothing else, in its creaturely or natural State, but a State of *Want*; and the *higher* its natural State is supposed to be, the higher is its Want, and the greater its Torment, if left only in its *natural* State. And this is the Reason of the excessive Misery and Depravity of the fallen Angels.

[Love-2.3-87] Now the *Contrariety* that is in *Desire,* and must be in it, because it is a Desire, and the only Ground of all Sensibility, is plainly shown you by the most undeniable Appearance in outward or material Nature. All that is done in outward Nature is done by the working of *Attraction*. And all Attraction is nothing else but an *inseparable* Combination and *incessant*

Working of *three contrary Properties,* or Laws of Motion. It draws, it resists its own Drawing; and from this Drawing and Resisting, which are necessarily *equal* to one another, it becomes an orbicular, or *whirling* Motion, and yet draws and resists, just as it did before.

[Love-2.3-88] Now this *threefold* Contrariety in the Motions, or Properties of Attraction, by which all the Elements of this material World are held and governed, and made to bring forth all the Wonders in all Kinds of animate and inanimate Things, this *Contrariety,* being the only possible *Ground* of all material Nature, is a full Demonstration, (1) That *Contrariety* is the one only possible Ground of Nature and all natural Life, whether it be eternal or temporal, spiritual or material; (2) That no *other Contrariety* is, or can be in the Properties or Laws of Attraction in this material Nature, but *that one* and the *same* Contrariety, which was from Eternity in spiritual Nature, is inseparable from it, and can be nowhere but in it. For Time can only partake of Eternity, it can have nothing in it but the Working of Eternity, nor be any Thing but what it is by the Working of Eternity in it. It can have nothing that is its own, or peculiar to it, but its transitory State, and Form, and Nature. It is a mere *Accident*, has only an *occasional* Existence; and whatever is seen, or done in it, is only so much of the *Working* of Eternity seen and done in it.

[Love-2.3-89] For Attraction, in the material World, has not only nothing material in it, but is impossible to be *communicated* to Matter; or rather Matter has no *possible Capacity* to receive Attraction. It can no more *receive* or *obey* the Laws of Attraction, than it can *make* Laws for Angels. It is as incapable of moving, or stirring itself, as it is of making Syllogisms. For Matter is, in itself, only Death, Darkness, and Inactivity, and is as utterly incapable of moving itself, as it is of illuminating or creating itself; nothing can be done in it, and by it, but that which is done by *something* that is not material.

[Love-2.3-90] Therefore, that which is called the Attraction of Materiality, is in itself nothing else but the Working of the *spiritual Properties* of Desire, which has in itself those *very three* inseparable Contrarieties, which make the three Contrarieties in the Motions of Attraction. Material Nature, being an *accidental, temporary, transitory* Out-Birth from eternal Nature, and having no Power of existing, but *under* it and in Dependence upon it, the spiritual Properties of eternal Nature do, as it were, *materialize* themselves for a Time, in their temporary Out-Birth and *force* Matter to work as they work, and to have the *same contradictory* Motions in it, which are essential to eternal Nature.

[Love-2.3-91] And thus the three inseparable, contrary Motions of Matter, are in the same Manner, and for the same Reason, a true Ground of a material Nature in Time, as the three inseparable, contrary, contradictory Workings of *Desire,* are a true Ground of *spiritual Nature* in Eternity. And you are to observe, that all that is done in *Matter* and *Time,* is done by the *same Agents,* or spiritual Properties, which do all that is *naturally* done in Eternity, in Heaven or in Hell. For nothing is the Ground of Happiness and Glory in Heaven, nothing is the Ground of Misery, Woe and Distraction in Hell, but the Working of these *same contrary Properties* of Desire, which work Contrariety in the Attraction of Matter and bring forth all the Changes of Life and Death in this material System. They are unchangeable in their Nature, and are everywhere the same; they are spiritual in Hell, and on Earth, as they are in Heaven. Considered as in themselves, they are everywhere equally good and equally bad; because they are everywhere equally the *Ground* and *only* the Ground for either Happiness or Misery. No possible Happiness, or Sensibility of Joy for any Creature, but where these *contrary* Properties work, nor any Possibility of Misery but from them.

[Love-2.3-92] Now *Attraction*, acting according to its three invariable, inseparable Contrarieties of Motion, stands in this material Nature, exactly in the *same Place* and for the same *End,* and doing the *same Office,* as the three first Properties of *Desire* do in eternal or spiritual Nature. For they can be, or do nothing with Regard to Earth and Time, but *that same* which they are, and do in Heaven and Eternity.

[Love-2.3-93] In eternal Nature, the three contrary Properties of Desire, answering exactly to the three contrary Motions of material Attraction, are in themselves only *Resistance, Rage*, and *Darkness,* and can be nothing else, till the *supernatural* Deity kindles its Fire of *Light* and *Love* in them; and then all their raging Contrarieties are changed into never-ceasing Sensibilities of Unity, Joy, and Happiness.

[Love-2.3-94] Just so, in this material System, suppose there to be nothing in it but the *contrary Motions* of Attraction, it could be nothing else but Rage against Rage in the Horror of Darkness.

[Love-2.3-95] But when the *same supernatural Light,* which turns the *first fighting* Properties of Nature into a Kingdom of Heaven, gives forth *something* of its Goodness into this World, through the kindled Body of the Sun, then all the fighting, contradictory Motions of Attraction, serve only to bring new Joys into the World, and open every Life, and every Blessing of Life, that can have Birth in a System of transitory Matter.

[Love-2.3-96] *Theogenes*. Oh *Theophilus*, you quite surprise me by thus showing me, with so much Certainty, how the Powers of Eternity work in the Things of Time. Nothing is done on Earth, but by the unchangeable Workings of the same spiritual Powers, which work after the same Manner, both in Heaven and in Hell. I now sufficiently see how Man stands in the midst of Heaven and Hell, under an absolute Necessity of belonging wholly to the one, or wholly to the other, as soon as this Cover of Materiality is taken off from him.

[Love-2.3-97] For *Matter* is his only Wall of Partition between them, he is equally nigh to both of them; and as Light and Love make all the Difference there is between Heaven and Hell, so nothing but a Birth of Light and Love in the Properties of his Soul, can possibly keep Hell out of it, or bring Heaven into it.

[Love-2.3-98] I now also see the full Truth and Certainty of what you said of the *Nature* and *Power* of Divine Love, *viz.,* "that it is perfect Peace and Joy, a Freedom from all Disquiet, making every Thing to rejoice in itself; that it is the Christ of God, and wherever it comes, it comes as the Blessing and Happiness of every natural Life; as the Restorer of every lost Perfection; a Redeemer from all Evil; a Fulfiller of all Righteousness; and a Peace of God, which passes all Understanding." So that I am now, a thousand Times more than ever, athirst after the Spirit of Love. I am willing to sell all, and buy it; its Blessing is so great, and the Want of it so dreadful a State, that I am even afraid of lying down in my Bed, till every working Power of my Soul is given up to it, wholly possessed and governed by it.

[Love-2.3-99] *Theophilus*. You have Reason for all that you say, *Theogenes*; for were we truly affected with Things, as they are our real Good or real Evil, we should be much more afraid of having the *Serpents* of Covetousness, Envy, Pride, and Wrath, well nourished and kept alive within us, than of being shut up in a Pest-house, or cast into a Dungeon of venomous Beasts. On the other Hand, we should look upon the lofty Eloquence, and proud Virtue of a *Cicero,* but as the Blessing of Storm and Tempest, when compared with the heavenly Tranquillity of that meek and lowly Heart, to which our Redeemer has called us.

[Love-2.3-100] I said the *Serpents* of Covetousness, Envy, Pride, and Wrath, because they are alone the *real, dreadful, original* Serpents; and all earthly Serpents are but transitory, partial, and weak Out-Births of them. All evil, earthly Beasts, are but short-lived Images, or creaturely Eruptions of that hellish Disorder, that is broken out from the fallen spiritual World; and by their manifold Variety, they show us that *Multiplicity* of Evil, that lies in the Womb of that Abyss of dark Rage, which (N.B.) has *no Maker*, but the three first Properties of Nature, fallen from God, and working in their Darkness.

[Love-2.3-101] So that all evil, mischievous, ravenous, venomous Beasts, though they have no Life, but what begins in and from this material World, and totally ends at the Death of their Bodies, yet have they no Malignity in their earthly, temporary Nature, but from those *same wrathful* Properties of fallen Nature, which live and work in our eternal fallen Souls. And therefore, though they are as different from us, as Time from Eternity, yet wherever we see them, we see so many infallible Proofs of the *Fall* of Nature, and the *Reality* of Hell. For was there no Hell broken out in spiritual Nature, not only no evil Beast, but no bestial Life, could ever have come into Existence.

[Love-2.3-102] For the Origin of Matter, and the bestial, earthly Life, stands thus. When the Fall of Angels had made their Dwelling-Place to be a dark Chaos of the first Properties of Nature left to themselves, the infinite Wisdom and Goodness of God created, or compacted this spiritual Chaos into a *material* Heaven, and a *material* Earth, and commanded the Light to enter into it. Hence this Chaos became the Ground, or the *Materiality* of a new and temporary Nature, in which the heavenly Power of Light, and the Properties of Darkness, each of them *materialized*, could work together, carrying on a War of Heaven against Earth; so that all the evil Workings of fallen spiritual Nature, and all the Good that was to overcome it, might be equally manifested both by the good and bad State of outward Nature, and by that Variety of good and bad living Creatures, that sprung up out of it; to stand in this State, *viz.,* of a *spiritual Chaos* changed into a *Materiality* of Light striving against Darkness, till the omnipotent Wisdom and Goodness of God, through the Wonders of a *first* and *second Adam*, shall have made this *Chaotic Earth* to send as many Angels into the highest Heaven, as fell with *Lucifer* into the hellish Chaos.

[Love-2.3-103] But to return. I have, I hope, sufficiently opened unto you the malignant Nature of *that Self,* which dwells in, and makes up the *working Life* of every Creature that has lost its *right State* in God; *viz.,* that all the Evil that was in the first Chaos of Darkness, or that still is in Hell and Devils, all the Evil that is in material Nature and material Creatures, whether animate, or inanimate, is nothing else, works in, and with nothing else, but those *first Properties* of Nature, which drive on the Life of fallen Man in Covetousness, Envy, Pride, and Wrath.

[Love-2.3-104] *Theogenes*. I could almost say, that you have shown me more than enough of this Monster of *Self*, though I would not be without this Knowledge of it for half the World. But now, Sir, what must I do to be saved from the Mouth of this *Lion*, for he is the Depth of all Subtlety, the *Satan* that deceiveth the whole World. He can hide himself under all *Forms* of Goodness, he can watch and fast, write and instruct, pray much, and preach long, give Alms to the Poor, visit the Sick, and yet often gets more Life and Strength, and a more immovable Abode, in these Forms of Virtue, than he has in Publicans and Sinners.

[Love-2.3-105] Enjoin me therefore whatever you please; all Rules, Methods, and Practices, will be welcome to me, if you judge them to be necessary in this Matter.

[Love-2.3-106] *Theophilus*. There is no need of a Number of Practices, or Methods in this Matter. For to die to Self, or to come from under its Power, is not, cannot be done by any *active* Resistance we can make to it by the Powers of Nature. For Nature can no more overcome or suppress itself, than Wrath can heal Wrath. So long as Nature acts, nothing but natural Works are brought forth; and therefore the more Labour of this Kind, the more Nature is fed and strengthened with its own Food.

[Love-2.3-107] But the *one true* Way of dying to Self is most *simple* and plain, it wants no Arts or Methods, no *Cells, Monasteries*, or *Pilgrimages*, it is equally practicable by every Body, it is always at Hand, it meets you in every Thing, it is free from all Deceit, and is never without Success.

[Love-2.3-108] If you ask, What is this one true, simple, plain, immediate and unerring Way? It is the Way of *Patience, Meekness, Humility*, and *Resignation* to God. This is the *Truth* and *Perfection* of dying to Self; it is nowhere else, nor possible to be in any Thing else, but in this State of Heart.

[Love-2.3-109] *Theogenes*. The Excellence and Perfection of these Virtues I readily acknowledge; but alas, Sir, how will this prove the Way of *overcoming Self* to be so *simple, plain, immediate*, and *unerring*, as you speak of? For is it not the Doctrine of almost all Men, and all Books, and confirmed by our own woeful Experience, that much Length of Time, and Exercise and Variety of Practices and Methods are necessary, and scarce sufficient to the Attainment of *any one* of these four Virtues?

[Love-2.3-110] *Theophilus*. When Christ our Saviour was upon Earth, was there any Thing more simple, plain, immediate, unerring, than the Way to Him? Did Scribes, Pharisees, Publicans, and Sinners, want any Length of Time, or Exercise of Rules and Methods, before they could have Admission to him, or have the Benefit of Faith in him?

[Love-2.3-111] *Theogenes*. I don't understand why you put this Question; nor do I see how it can possibly relate to the Matter before us.

[Love-2.3-112] *Theophilus*. It not only relates to, but is the very *Heart* and *Truth* of the Matter before us: It is not appealed to, by Way of Illustration of our Subject, but is our Subject itself, only set in a truer and stronger Light. For when I refer you to Patience, Meekness, Humility, and

Resignation to God, as the one simple, plain, immediate, and unerring Way of dying to Self, or being saved from it, I call it so for no other Reason, but because you can as *easily* and *immediately*, without Art or Method, by the mere Turning and Faith of your Mind, have all the Benefit of these Virtues, as Publicans and Sinners, by their turning to Christ, could be helped and saved by him.

[Love-2.3-113] *Theogenes*. But, good Sir, would you have me then believe, that my *turning* and *giving* up myself to these Virtues is as certain and immediate a Way of my being directly possessed and blessed by their good Power, as when Sinners turned to Christ to be helped and saved by him? Surely this is too short a Way, and has too much of Miracle in it, to be now expected.

[Love-2.3-114] *Theophilus*. I would have you strictly to believe all this, in the fullest Sense of the Words, and also to believe, that the Reasons why you, or any others are for a long Time vainly endeavouring after, and hardly ever attaining these First-rate Virtues, is because you seek them in the Way they are not to be found, in a *Multiplicity* of human Rules, Methods, and Contrivances, and not in that *Simplicity* of Faith, in which, those who applied to Christ, immediately obtained that which they asked of Him.

[Love-2.3-115] "Come unto me, all ye that labour and are heavy laden, and I will refresh you." How short and simple and certain a Way to Peace and Comfort, from the Misery and Burden of Sin! What becomes now of your Length of Time and Exercise, your Rules and Methods, and round-about Ways, to be delivered from Self, the Power of Sin, and find the redeeming Power and Virtue of Christ? Will you say, that turning to Christ in Faith was *once* indeed the Way for Jews and Heathens to enter into Life, and be delivered from the Power of their Sins, but that all this Happiness was at an End, as soon as *Pontius Pilate* had nailed this good Redeemer to the Cross, and so broken off all *immediate* Union and Communion between Faith and Christ?

[Love-2.3-116] What a Folly would it be to suppose, that Christ, after his having finished his great Work, overcome Death, ascended into Heaven, with all Power in Heaven and on Earth, was become less a Saviour and gave less certain and immediate Helps to those, that by Faith turn to him now, than when he was clothed with the Infirmity of our Flesh and Blood upon Earth? Has He less Power, after he has conquered, than whilst he was only resisting and fighting our Enemies? Or has He less good Will to assist his Church, his own Body, now he is in Heaven, than he had to assist Publicans, Sinners, and Heathens before he was glorified, as the Redeemer of the World? And yet this must be the Case, if our *simply turning* to Him in Faith and Hope, is not as sure a Way of obtaining immediate Assistance from him now, as when he was upon Earth.

[Love-2.3-117] *Theogenes*. You seem, Sir, to me to have stepped aside from the Point in Question, which was not, Whether my turning or giving myself up to Christ, in Faith in him, would not do me as much Good as it did to them, who turned to him when He was upon Earth? But whether my turning in Faith and Desire, to *Patience, Meekness, Humility*, and *Resignation* to God, would do all that as fully for me now, as Faith in Christ did for those who became his Disciples?

[Love-2.3-118] *Theophilus*. I have stuck closely, my Friend, to the Point before us. Let it be supposed, that I had given you a Form of Prayer in these Words. *O Lamb of God*, that takest away the Sins of the World; Or, O *Thou Bread that camest down from Heaven*; Or, Thou *that art the Resurrection, and the Life*, the *Light* and *Peace* of all holy Souls, help me to a living Faith in Thee. Would you say, that this was not a Prayer of Faith in and to Christ, because it did not call Him *Jesus*, or the *Son of God*? Answer me plainly.

[Love-2.3-119] *Theogenes*. What can I answer you, but that this is a most true and good Prayer to Jesus, the Son of the living God? For who else but He was the *Lamb* of God, and the *Bread* that came down?

[Love-2.3-120] *Theophilus*. Well answered, my Friend. When therefore I exhort you to give up yourself in Faith and Hope, to *Patience, Meekness, Humility*, and *Resignation to God*, what else do I do, but turn you directly to *so much* Faith and Hope in the true Lamb of God? For if I ask you, what the Lamb of God is, and means, must you not tell me, that it is, and means, the *Perfection* of Patience, Meekness, Humility, and Resignation to God? Can you say, it is either more or less than this? Must you not therefore say, that a Faith of Hunger and Thirst, and Desire of these Virtues, is in Spirit and Truth, the one *very same* Thing, as a Faith of Hunger and Thirst, and Desire of Salvation through the Lamb of God? And consequently, that every sincere Wish and Desire, every inward Inclination of your Heart, that presses after these Virtues, and longs to be governed by them, is an *immediate direct* Application to Christ, is *worshipping* and *falling down* before him, is *giving up* yourself unto him, and the very *Perfection* of Faith in him?

[Love-2.3-121] If you distrust my Words, hear the Words of Christ himself. "Learn of me," says He, "for I am meek and lowly of Heart, and ye shall find Rest unto your Souls." Here you have the plain Truth of our two Points fully asserted, *First*, That to be *given up to*, or stand in a *Desire* of, Patience, Meekness, Humility, and Resignation to God, is strictly the *same Thing*, as to learn of Christ, or to have Faith in Him. *Secondly*, That this is the *one simple, short*, and *infallible* Way to overcome, or be delivered from all the Malignity and Burden of *Self* expressed in these Words, "and ye shall find Rest unto your Souls."

[Love-2.3-122] And all this, because this simple Tendency, or inward Inclination of your Heart to *sink down* into Patience, Meekness, Humility, and Resignation to God, is truly giving up all that you are, and all that you have from fallen *Adam*; it is perfectly leaving all that you have, to follow and be with Christ, it is your highest Act of Faith in him and Love of Him, the most ardent and earnest Declaration of your cleaving to him with all your Heart, and seeking for no Salvation but in him, and from him. And therefore all the Good, and Blessing, Pardon, and Deliverance from Sin that ever happened to anyone from any Kind, or Degree of Faith and Hope, and Application to Christ, is sure to be had from this State of Heart, which stands continually *turned to him* in a Hunger, and Desire, of being led and governed by his Spirit of Patience, Meekness, Humility, and Resignation to God. Oh *Theogenes*, could I help you to perceive or feel what a Good there is in this State of Heart; you would Desire it with more Eagerness, than the thirsty Hart desireth the Water-Brooks, you would think of nothing, desire nothing, but constantly to live in it. It is a Security from all Evil, and all Delusion; no Difficulty, or Trial, either of Body or Mind, no Temptation either within you, or without you, but what has its full Remedy in this State of Heart. You have no Questions to ask of any Body, no new Way that you need inquire after; no Oracle that you need to consult; for whilst you shut up yourself in Patience, Meekness, Humility, and Resignation to God, you are in the very Arms of Christ, your whole Heart is his Dwelling-Place, and He lives and works in you, as certainly as he lived in, and governed that Body and Soul, which he took from the Virgin *Mary*.

[Love-2.3-123] Learn whatever else you will from Men and Books, or even from Christ Himself, besides, or without these Virtues, and you are only a poor Wanderer in a barren Wilderness, where no Water of Life is to be found. For Christ is nowhere, but in these Virtues, and where they are, there is He in his own Kingdom. From Morning to Night, let this be the Christ that you follow, and then you will fully escape all the religious Delusions that are in the World, and what is more, all the Delusions of your own selfish Heart.

[Love-2.3-124] For to seek to be saved by Patience, Meekness, Humility, and Resignation to God, is truly coming to God through Christ; and when these Tempers live and abide in you, as the Spirit and Aim of your Life, then Christ is in you of a Truth, and the Life that you then lead, is not yours, but it is Christ that liveth in you. For this is following Christ with all your Power: You cannot possibly make more Haste after Him, you have no other Way of walking as he walked, no other Way of being like Him, of truly believing in him, of showing your Trust in him, and Dependence upon him, but by wholly giving up yourself to *That,* which He was, *viz.,* to Patience, Meekness, Humility, and Resignation to God.

[Love-2.3-125] Tell me now, have I enough proved to you, the short, simple, and certain Way of destroying that Body of Self, which lives and works in the four Elements of *Covetousness, Envy, Pride,* and *Wrath*?

[Love-2.3-126] *Theogenes.* Enough of all Reason. But as to *Covetousness,* I thank God, I cannot charge myself with it, it has no Power over me, nay I naturally abhor it. And I also now clearly see, why I have been so long struggling in vain against other selfish Tempers.

[Love-2.3-127] *Theophilus.* Permit me, my Friend, to remove your Mistake. Had Covetousness, no Power over you, you could have no other *selfish* Tempers to struggle against. They are all dead, as soon as Covetousness has done working in you. You take Covetousness to relate only to the Wealth of this World. But this is but *one single* Branch of it, its Nature is as large as Desire, and wherever selfish Desire is, there is all the evil Nature of Covetousness.

[Love-2.3-128] Now Envy, Pride, Hatred, or Wrath, can have no Possibility of Existence in you, but because there is *some selfish Desire* alive in you, that is not *satisfied,* not *gratified,* but *resisted* or *disappointed*. And therefore so long as any selfish Tempers, whether of Envy, Uneasiness, Complaint, Pride, or Wrath, are alive in you, you have the fullest Proof, that all these Tempers are *born* and *bred* in and from your *own Covetousness,* that is, from that same *selfish bad Desire,* which when it is turned to the Wealth of this World is called Covetousness. For all these four Elements of Self, or fallen Nature, are tied together in one inseparable Band, they mutually generate, and are generated from one another, they have but one common Life, and must all of them live, or all die together. This may show you again the absolute Necessity of our *one simple* and *certain* Way of dying to Self, and the *absolute Insufficiency* of all human Means whatever to effect it.

[Love-2.3-129] For consider only this, that to be *angry* at our own Anger, to be *ashamed* of our own Pride, and *strongly* resolve not to be *weak*, is the Upshot of all *human Endeavours*; and yet all this is rather the Life, than the Death of Self. There is no Help, but from a *total Despair* of all human Help. When a Man is brought to such an inward full Conviction, as to have no more Hope from all human Means, than he hopes to see with his Hands, or hear with his Feet, then it is, that he is truly prepared to die to Self, that is, to give up all Thoughts of having or doing any Thing that is good, in any *other Way* but that of a meek, humble, patient, total Resignation of himself to God. All that we do before *this Conviction,* is in great Ignorance of ourselves, and full of Weakness and Impurity. Let our Zeal be ever so wonderful, yet if it begins sooner, or proceeds further, or to any other Matter, or in any other Way, than as it is led and guided by this Conviction, it is full of Delusion. No Repentance, however long or laborious, is *Conversion* to God, till it falls into this State. For God must do all, or all is nothing; but God cannot do all, till all is expected from Him; and all is not expected from Him, till by a true and *good Despair* of every human Help, we have no Hope, or Trust, or Longing after any Thing but a patient, meek, humble, total Resignation to God.

[Love-2.3-130] And now, my dear Friends, I have brought you to the very Place for which I desired this Day's Conversation; which was, to set your Feet upon sure Ground, with Regard to the *Spirit of Love*. For all that Variety of Matters through which we have passed, has been only a Variety of Proofs, that the *Spirit* of Divine Love can have no Place, or Possibility of Birth in any fallen Creature, till it wills and *chooses* to be dead to *all Self,* in a patient, meek, humble Resignation to the good Power and Mercy of God.

[Love-2.3-131] And from this State of Heart also it is, that the *Spirit* of Prayer is born, which is the Desire of the Soul turned to God. Stand, therefore, steadfastly in *this Will*, let nothing else enter into your Mind, have no other Contrivance, but everywhere, and in every Thing, to nourish and keep up *this State* of Heart, and then your House is built upon a Rock; you are safe from all Danger; the Light of Heaven, and the Love of God, will begin their Work in you, will bless and sanctify every Power of your fallen Soul; you will be in a Readiness for every Kind of Virtue and good Work, and will know what it is to be led by the Spirit of God.

[Love-2.3-132] *Theogenes*. But, dear *Theophilus*, though I am so delighted with what you say, that I am loath to stop you, yet permit me to mention a Fear that rises up in me. Suppose I should find myself so overcome with my own Darkness and selfish Tempers, as not to be able to *sink* from them into a Sensibility of this meek, humble, patient, full Resignation to God, what must I then do, or how shall I have the Benefit of what you have taught me?

[Love-2.3-133] *Theophilus*. You are then at the very Time and Place of receiving the fullest Benefit from it, and practicing it with the greatest Advantage to yourself. For though this patient, meek Resignation is to be exercised with Regard to all outward Things, and Occurrences of Life, yet it chiefly respects our own inward State, the Troubles, Perplexities, Weaknesses, and Disorders of our own fallen Souls. And to stand *turned* to a patient, meek, humble Resignation to God, when your own Impatience, Wrath, Pride, and Irresignation, attack yourself, is a higher and more beneficial Performance of this Duty, than when you stand turned to Meekness and Patience, when attacked by the Pride, or Wrath, or disorderly Passions of other People. I say, *stand turned* to this patient, humble Resignation, for this is your true Performance of this Duty at that Time; and though you may have no comfortable *Sensibility* of your performing it, yet in this State you may always have *one full Proof* of the Truth and Reality of it, and that is, when you seek for Help no other Way, nor in any Thing else, neither from Men nor Books, but wholly leave and give up yourself to be helped by the Mercy of God. And thus, be your State what it will, you may always have the *full Benefit* of this short and sure Way of resigning up yourself to God. And the greater the Perplexity of your Distress is, the nearer you are to the greatest and best Relief, provided you have but *Patience* to expect it *all* from God. For nothing brings you so near to Divine Relief, as the *Extremity* of Distress; for the Goodness of God hath no other *Name* or *Nature,* but the Helper of all that wants to be helped; and nothing can possibly hinder your finding this Goodness of God, and every other Gift and Grace that you stand in Need of; nothing can hinder or delay it, but your *turning from* the only Fountain of Life and living Water, to some cracked Cistern of your own Making; to this or that *Method, Opinion, Division,* or *Subdivision* amongst Christians, carnally expecting some mighty Things either from *Samaria,* or *Jerusalem, Paul* or *Apollos*, which are only and solely to be had by worshipping the Father in Spirit and in Truth, which is then only done, when your whole Heart and Soul and Spirit trusts *wholly* and *solely* to the *Operation* of that God within you, in whom we live, move, and have our Being. And be assured of this, as a most certain Truth, that we have neither more nor less of the Divine Operation within us, because of this or that outward Form, or Manner of our Life, but *just* and *strictly* in that Degree, as our Faith, and Hope, and Trust, and Dependence upon God, are more or less in us.

[Love-2.3-134] What a Folly then to be so often perplexed about the Way to God? For nothing is the Way to God, but our Heart. God is nowhere else to be found; and the Heart itself cannot find Him, or be helped by any Thing else to find Him, but by its *own Love* of Him, *Faith* in Him, *Dependence* upon Him, *Resignation* to Him, and *Expectation* of all from Him.

[Love-2.3-135] These are short, but full *Articles* of true Religion, which carry Salvation along with them, which make a true and full Offering and Oblation of our whole Nature to the *Divine Operation,* and also a true and full Confession of the Holy Trinity in Unity. For as they look wholly to the *Father,* as blessing us with the *Operation* of his *own Word,* and *Spirit,* so they truly confess, and worship the *holy Trinity* of God. And as they ascribe all to, and expect all from this Deity *alone*, so they make the *truest* and *best* of all Confessions, that there is no God but one.

[Love-2.3-136] Let then *Arians, Semi-Arians*, and *Socinians,* who puzzle their laborious Brains to make Paper-Images of a Trinity for themselves, have nothing from you but your Pity and Prayers; your Foundation standeth sure, whilst you look for all your Salvation through the *Father,* working Life in your Soul by his *own Word,* and *Spirit,* which dwell in Him, and are one Life, both in Him and you.

[Love-2.3-137] *Theogenes*. I can never enough thank you, *Theophilus*, for this good and comfortable Answer to my scrupulous Fear. It seems now, as if I could always know how to find full Relief in this humble, meek, patient, total Resignation of myself to God. It is, as you said, a Remedy that is always at hand, equally practicable at all Times, and never in greater Reality, than when my own Tempers are making War against it in my own Heart.

[Love-2.3-138] You have quite carried your Point with me. The God of Patience, Meekness, and Love, is the one God of my Heart. It is now the whole Bent and Desire of my Soul, to seek for all my Salvation in and through the *Merits* and *Mediation* of the meek, humble, patient, resigned, suffering Lamb of God, who alone hath Power to bring forth the blessed Birth of these heavenly Virtues in my Soul. He is the Bread of God, that came down from Heaven, of which the Soul must eat, or perish and pine in everlasting Hunger. He is the *Eternal Love* and *Meekness,* that left the Bosom of his Father, to be Himself the Resurrection of Meekness and Love in all the darkened, wrathful Souls of fallen Men. What a Comfort is it, to think that this Lamb of God, Son of the Father, Light of the World, who is the Glory of Heaven, and Joy of Angels, is as near to us, as truly in the midst of us, as he is in the midst of Heaven; and that not a Thought, Look, and Desire of our Heart, that presses toward Him, longing to catch, as it were, one small Spark of his heavenly Nature, but is in as sure a Way of finding Him, touching Him, and drawing Virtue from Him as the Woman who was healed, by longing but to touch the Border of his Garment.

[Love-2.3-139] This Doctrine also makes me quite weary and ashamed of all my own natural Tempers, as so Many Marks of the Beast upon me; every Whisper of my Soul that stirs up Impatience, Uneasiness, Resentment, Pride, and Wrath within me, shall be rejected with a *Get thee behind me, Satan*, for it is his, and has its whole Nature from him. To rejoice in a Resentment gratified, appears now to me to be quite frightful. For what is it, in reality, but rejoicing that my *own Serpent* of Self has new Life and Strength given to it, and that the precious Lamb of God is denied Entrance into my Soul. For this is the strict Truth of the Matter. To give into Resentment, and go willingly to gratify it, is calling up the Courage of your own Serpent, and truly helping it to be more stout and valiant, and successful in you.— On the other Hand, to give up all Resentment of every Kind, and on every Occasion, however artfully, beautifully, outwardly coloured, and to sink down into the Humility of Meekness under all Contrariety, Contradiction, and Injustice, always turning the other Cheek to the Smiter, however haughty, is the best of all Prayers, the surest of all Means to have nothing but Christ living and working in you, as the Lamb of God, that taketh away every Sin that ever had Power over your Soul.

[Love-2.3-140] What a Blindness was it in me, to think that I had no Covetousness because the Love of Pelf *{money or gain}*, was not felt by me! For to covet, is to desire. And what can it signify whether I desire This or That? If I desire any Thing but that which God would have me to be and do, I stick in the Mire of Covetousness, and must have all that Evil and Disquiet living and working in me, which robs *Misers* of their Peace both with God and Man.

[Love-2.3-141] Oh sweet Resignation of myself to God, happy Death of every selfish Desire, blessed Unction of a holy Life, the only Driver of all Evil out of my Soul, be thou my Guide and Governor wherever I go! Nothing but thou can take me from myself, nothing but thou can lead me to God; Hell has no Power where thou art; nor can Heaven hide itself from thee. Oh may I never indulge a Thought, bring forth a Word, or do any Thing for myself or others, but under the Influence of thy blessed Inspiration!

[Love-2.3-142] Forgive, dear *Theophilus*, this Transport of my Soul; I could not stop it. The Sight, though distant, of this heavenly *Canaan*, this *Sabbath* of the Soul, freed from the miserable Labour of Self, to rest in Meekness, Humility, Patience, and Resignation under the

Spirit of God, is like the joyful Voice of the Bridegroom to my Soul, and leaves no Wish in me, but to be at the Marriage Feast of the Lamb.

[Love-2.3-143] *Theophilus.* Thither, *Theogenes,* you must certainly come, if you keep to the Path of Meekness, Humility, and Patience, under a full Resignation to God. But if you go aside from it, let the Occasion seem ever so glorious, or the Effects ever so wonderful to you, it is only preparing for yourself a *harder Death.* For die you must to all, and every Thing that you have worked or done under any other Spirit, but that of Meekness, Humility, and true Resignation to God. Every Thing else, be it what it will, hath its Rise from the Fire of *Nature,* it belongs to nothing else, and must of all Necessity be given up, lost, and taken from you again by *Fire,* either here or hereafter.

[Love-2.3-144] For these Virtues are the only *Wedding Garment*; they are the *Lamps* and *Vessels* well furnished with Oil.

[Love-2.3-145] There is nothing that will do in the Stead of them; they must have their *own full* and *perfect* Work in you, if not before, yet certainly after the Death of the Body, or the Soul can never be delivered from its fallen wrathful State. And all this is no more than is implied in this Scripture Doctrine, *viz.,* that there is no Possibility of Salvation, but in and by a Birth of the meek, humble, patient, resigned Lamb of God in our Souls. And when this Lamb of God has brought forth a real Birth of his own Meekness, Humility, and full Resignation to God in our Souls, then are our Lamps trimmed, and our Virgin-hearts made ready for the Marriage Feast.

[Love-2.3-146] This *Marriage Feast* signifies the *Entrance* into the highest State of *Union,* that can be between God and the Soul, in this Life. Or in other Words, it is the Birth-Day of the Spirit of Love in our Souls, which whenever we attain it, will feast our Souls with such Peace and Joy in God, as will blot out the Remembrance of every Thing, that we called Peace or Joy before.

[Love-2.3-147] In the *Letter* on the Spirit of Love, you have been shown, according to the *Mystery* of all Things opened by the Goodness of God in the blessed *Behmen,* the *Time* and *Place* of its Birth. That it neither does, nor can possibly begin any sooner, than at the *Entrance* or *Manifestation* of the Divine Light, in the *three first* wrathful, self-tormenting Properties of Nature, which are and must be the Ground of every natural Life, and must be Darkness, Rage, and Torment, till the Light of God, breaking in upon them, changes all their painful working into the strongest Sensibilities of Love, Joy, and Triumph, in the Perception and Possession of a new Divine Life.

[Love-2.3-148] Now all that we have said To-day of the Necessity of the fallen Souls *dying to Self,* by *Meekness, Patience, Humility, and full Resignation to God* is strictly the same Thing, and asserted from the *same Ground* as when it was then said, that the *three first* Properties of Nature must have their wrathful Activity taken from them, by the Light of God breaking in upon them, or manifesting itself in them. Now this was always the State of Nature, it never was a State of Wrath, because it never was without the Light of God in it. But the natural, creaturely Life, having a Possibility of falling, and having actually fallen from God, has found and felt what never ought to have been found and felt, *viz.,* what Nature is in itself, without the Manifestation of the Deity in it.

[Love-2.3-149] Therefore, as sure as the Light of God, or the Entrance of the Deity into the *three first* Properties of Nature, is absolutely necessary to make Nature to be a heavenly Kingdom of Light and Love, so sure and certain is it, that the creaturely Life, that is fallen from God under the wrathful *first Properties* of Nature, can have no Deliverance from it, cannot have a Birth of heavenly Light and Love, by any other possible Way, but that of dying to Self, by Meekness, Humility, Patience, and full Resignation to God.

[Love-2.3-150] And the Reason is this. It is because the *Will* is the Leader of the creaturely Life, and it can have nothing but *that* to which its Will is *turned*. And therefore it cannot be saved from, or raised out of the Wrath of Nature, till its Will *turns* from Nature, and wills to be no longer driven by it. But it cannot *turn* from Nature, or show a *Will* to come from under its Power, any *other Way,* than by turning and giving up itself to that Meekness, Humility, Patience, and Resignation to God, which so far as it goes, is a *leaving, rejecting*, and *dying* to all the Guidance of Nature.

[Love-2.3-151] And thus you see, that this *one simple* Way is, according to the immutable Nature of Things, the *one only possible* and absolutely *necessary* Way to God. It is as possible to go two contrary Ways at once, as to go to God any other Way than this. But what is best of all, this Way is absolutely *infallible*; nothing can defeat it. And all this infallibility is fully grounded in the two-fold Character of our Saviour (1) As he is the *Lamb of God*, a Principle, and Source of all Meekness, and Humility in the Soul, and (2) As he is the *Light of Eternity,* that blesses eternal Nature, and turns it into a Kingdom of Heaven.

[Love-2.3-152] For in this two-fold Respect, he has a Power of redeeming us, which nothing can hinder; but sooner or later, he must see all his and our Enemies under his Feet, and all that is fallen in *Adam* into Death must rise and return to a Unity of an Eternal Life in God.

[Love-2.3-153] For, as the Lamb of God, he has *all Power* to bring forth in us a *Sensibility* and a Weariness of our own wrathful State, and a Willingness to fall from it into Meekness, Humility, Patience, and Resignation to that Mercy of God which alone can help us. And when we are thus weary and heavy laden, and willing to get Rest to our Souls, in meek, humble, patient Resignation to God, then it is, that He, as the *Light of God* and Heaven, joyfully breaks in upon us, turns our Darkness into Light, our Sorrow into Joy, and begins that Kingdom of God and Divine Love within us which will never have an End.

[Love-2.3-154] Need I say more, *Theogenes*, to show you how to come out of the Wrath of your evil earthly Nature, into the sweet Peace and Joy of the Spirit of Love? Neither Notions, nor Speculations, nor Heat, nor Fervour, nor Rules, nor Methods can bring it forth. It is the *Child* of Light, and cannot possibly have any Birth in you, but only and solely from the *Light* of God rising in your own Soul, as it rises in heavenly Beings. But the Light of God cannot *arise,* or be *found* in you, by any Art or Contrivance of your own, but *only* and *solely* in the Way of that Meekness, Humility, and Patience, which waits, trusts, resigns to, and expects all from the inward, living, life-giving Operation of the Triune God within you, creating, quickening, and reviving in your fallen Soul that Birth and Image, and Likeness of the Holy Trinity, in which the first Father of Mankind was created.

[Love-2.3-155] *Theogenes.* You need say no more, *Theophilus*; you have not only removed that Difficulty which brought us hither, but have, by a Variety of Things, fixed and confirmed us in a full Belief of that great truth elsewhere asserted, namely "That there is but one Salvation for all Mankind, and that is the *Life of God* in the Soul. And also, that there is but *one possible* Way for Man to attain this Life of God, not one for a *Jew*, another for a *Christian*, and a third for a *Heathen*. No, God is one, and the Way to it is one, and that is, the *Desire* of the Soul turned to God."

[Love-2.3-156] Therefore, dear *Theophilus*, adieu. If we see you no more in this Life, you have sufficiently taught us how to seek, and find every kind of Goodness, Blessing, and Happiness, in God alone.

CPSIA information can be obtained
at www.ICGtesting.com
Printed in the USA
LVHW08s1800140818
586952LV00025B/852/P